RULING SHAIKHS
and
HER MAJESTY'S GOVERNMENT
1960–1969

RULING SHAIKHS

and

HER MAJESTY'S GOVERNMENT

1960–1969

MIRIAM JOYCE

Purdue University, Calumet

Foreword by
Sir Donald Hawley

FRANK CASS
LONDON • PORTLAND, OR

First published in 2003 in Great Britain by
FRANK CASS PUBLISHERS
Crown House, 47 Chase Side, Southgate
London N14 5BP

and in the United States of America by
FRANK CASS PUBLISHERS
c/o ISBS, 5824 N.E. Hassalo Street
Portland, Oregon, 97213-3644

Website: www.frankcass.com

British Library Cataloguing in Publication Data

Joyce, Miriam
Ruling Shaikhs and Her Majesty's Government 1960–1969
1. Great Britain – Foreign relations – Persian Gulf States
2. Great Britain – Foreign relations – 1945–1964 3. Great Britain – Foreign
relations – 1964–1979 4. Persian Gulf States – Foreign relations – Great Britain
I. Title
327.4'1'0536'09046

ISBN 0-7146-5413-2

Library of Congress Cataloging-in-Publication Data

Joyce, Miriam
Ruling Shaikhs and Her Majesty's Government 1960–1969/Miriam, Joyce.
    p. cm.
Includes bibliographical references (p.) and index.
ISBN 0-7146-5413-2 (cloth)
    1. Persian Gulf States–Relations–Great Britain 2. Great
Britain–Relations–Persian Gulf States. I. Title.

DS247.A138J69 2003
327'.09536–dc21

2002041496

Typeset in 11/13pt Janson by FiSH Books, London WC1
Printed in Great Britain by MPG Books
Victoria Square
Bodmin, Cornwall

In honor of
my granddaughter Lily Eva and her parents
Adam and Judy Haron

Contents

Maps

Foreword

Miriam Joyce has chosen to write about a crucial period in Gulf history. The political scene in the Gulf of the 1960s was beginning to become more complex. It was still dominated by Britain, the old Protecting Power, which continued to develop its relations based on early 19th century treaties with the Shaikhdoms – and with the Sultanate of Muscat and Oman albeit in a different way as it was never formally 'Protected'. There was no pressure from the Rulers and their governments for any major changes in their long-standing relationships.

Increasing oil finds and revenues, however, gave the Gulf states an importance they previously lacked and rapidly changed their peoples' standard of living and of modern sophistication. Two different centres of Arab nationalism, Cairo and Baghdad, competed for influence, with the Egypt of Gemal Abdel Nasser in the ascendant. As the decade advanced, Arab revolutionary movements particularly those based in Aden and south Yemen and supported in various degrees by Baghdad, China, East Germany and the Soviet Union sought to shake the essential stability of the Gulf. The Peoples Front for the Liberation of Oman and the Arabian Gulf even stated their purpose in their title. The very name of the Gulf became a contentious issue and the strongest power in the area, Iran, confident under the Shah and retentive of the historically established title of Persian Gulf – sought closer bilateral relations with the Arab states of the southern Gulf based on long-standing custom and propinquity. An announcement by the British Government in January 1968 dramatically changed the picture. Britain was to abandon the former bipartisan policy of direct military support for the Shaikhdoms and also, at the end of 1971, to end the Treaties of Protection as part of a strategic decision to withdraw from all military commitments East of Suez. This sudden change of policy came as a deep shock to the Rulers and Sultan and was the more unwelcome and unexpected as only two months earlier British Ministers had assured them that, despite her withdrawal from Aden, Britain would continue to fulfil her treaty obligations to them.

This was the second fundamental decision by a Labour Government to accelerate events and reduce Britain's responsibilities overseas, the first example having been India immediately after the 1939–1945 war. The reasons for the 1968 declaration which was incidentally as unpopular at the time with Malaysia and Singapore as it was with Gulf Rulers – were stated to be economic. It is perhaps ironical, therefore, that at the moment of writing, the present Labour Government is preparing for fresh involvement in the region in alliance with the United States.

Unsettling as it was, the announcement nonetheless certainly precipitated new thinking and, amongst such new thoughts, the concept of a possible federation of nine states, the seven Trucial States with Bahrain and Qatar, was born. In the event Bahrain and Qatar became independent states in 1971, when a federation of the seven formed the present United Arab Emirates. It was always the more logical outcome and was already being discussed seriously when I was Political Agent between 1958 and 1961, although it was not then a practical possibility.

This book shows how the United Arab Emirates actually came to be formed following an historic accord between Shaikh Zayyed bin Sultan of Abu Dhabi and Shaikh Rashid bin Said of Dubai. The modern Gulf, however, only took shape after three prominent characters, Shaikh Shakhbut bin Sultan, Ruler of Abu Dhabi, Shaikh Saqr bin Sultan of Sharjah and, later in 1970, the Sultan of Muscat and Oman, were deposed at the instigation of their families on the grounds that they would not face the realities of the modern world soon enough.

The contemporary sources drawn on by Miriam Joyce give interesting insights into these matters and many other aspects of Gulf affairs during the period, including the last years of Sultan Said bin Taimur before Sultan Qaboos took over and what others thought about his character and integrity. Valuable light is also thrown on the special case of Kuwait and its relations with Iraq and the general attitude of the United States to the region. The US are shown to have had no intention at the time of replacing Britain as 'policeman' of the Gulf. Incidentally I had personal confirmation of this.

In 1971 I became the first Ambassador accredited to Sultan Qaboos and my US colleague, who was the next to present his credentials in 1972 – told me that the US was happy to leave the main political running in the area to Britain as long as we had the will to be actively involved. 'Commercially', he added significantly 'we are rivals'.

The Gulf Shaikhdoms and the Sultanate of Oman smoothly and successfully overcame any difficulties caused by the British withdrawal and, since then, have remained essentially stable. They have, moreover, with their traditional rulers gradually introducing more representative institutions suited to their own environments, outlasted some of the full-blown democracies of the Westminster model introduced in countries elsewhere. It remains to be seen whether the flexibility and often inventiveness – of these traditionally based Arab societies may yet prove more enduring than other models advocated by the West as progressive.

Donald Hawley

Acknowledgements

Much of the research for this book was completed during my sabbatical year. I appreciate the continuing support of my department chairman, Saul Lerner, and the assistance of our patient secretary, Kris Mihalic.

During the course of my travels I enjoyed the hospitality of numerous friends. I am grateful to them all, especially to Ruthy and Leslie Greenfield in Ramat HaSharon, Irit and Beni Dagan, Jerri and Stanley Kovell in Washington. Finally, I am indebted to Judith Becker Thomas who arrived in London to assist in my departure from a dreadful flat on Curzon Street.

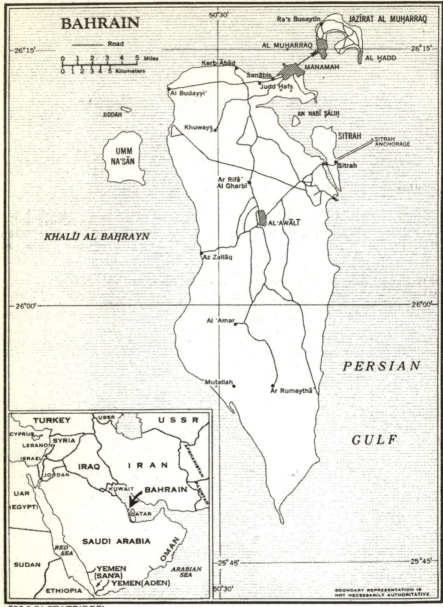

290 9-71 STATE(RGE)

Reproduced from the collections of The Library of Congress,
Geography and Map Division

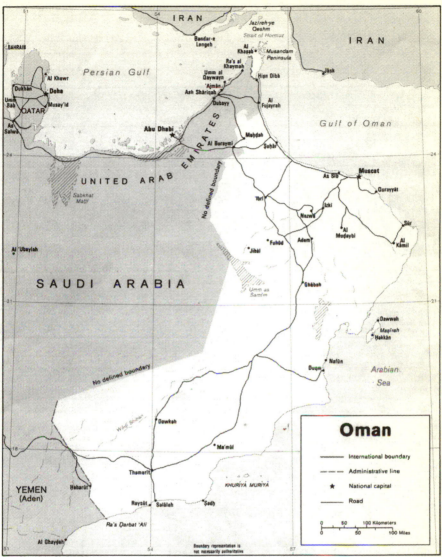

Oman

— International boundary
--- --- Administrative line
★ National capital
—— Road

Base 504162 11-79 (544486)

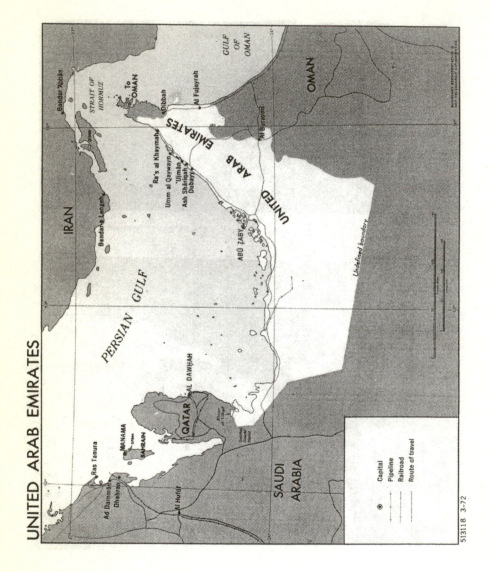

Reproduced from the collections of The Library of Congress,
Geography and Map Division

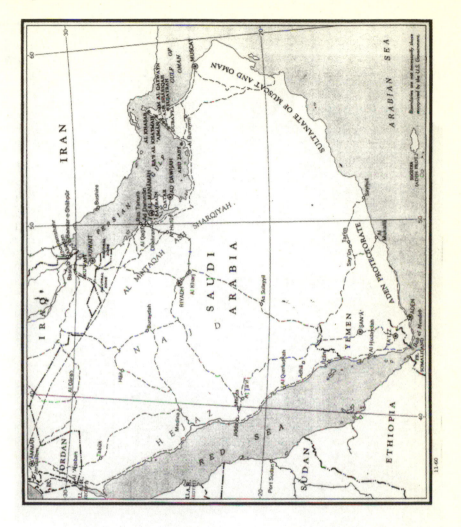

Arabian Peninsula (4 May 1961)

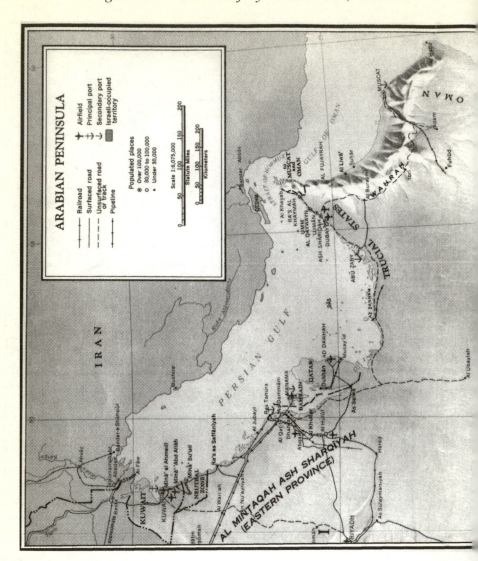

Arabian Peninsula (4 March 1970)

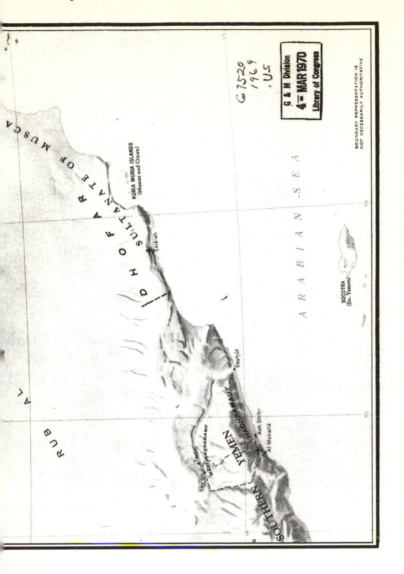

Arabian Peninsula (4 March 1970)

Introduction

Initially, Britain's interest in the Persian/Arab Gulf region was strictly commercial. In 1616, under a *firman* issued by Shah Abbas, the English East India Company received the right to trade and established facilities in Bandar Abbas. But in 1763, the company transferred operations to Basra, where a satellite office had already operated for 40 years. At the same time, the company opened a branch in Bushire.[1] As British trade with India expanded, the East India Company became increasingly concerned with the suppression of piracy in the Gulf. As a result, the British government sent expeditions against the Trucial Coast. The superiority of Britian's naval forces ended piracy and led to the signing of treaties between the British government and some of the coastal shaikhs.[2]

In 1839, Britain captured the port of Aden and established a colony there, which became an important naval base and, in 1869, after the opening of the Suez Canal, a refueling port for ships sailing to India. Throughout the nineteenth century, as the British extended their empire, London's interest in the Gulf increased. As a result, Britain continued to sign protection treaties with many of the region's tribal leaders; treaties that recognized the sovereignty of the ruler and stipulated that the shaikhs agreed to permit British control of their foreign relations. Gulf rulers also agreed that they would neither cede territory nor make treaties without first obtaining British permission. At the same time, the British attempted, not always successfully, to refrain from meddling in tribal issues. In 1856, the Acting Political Resident in the Gulf explained that the British never interfered in internal affairs, but 'should their quarrels extend to the sea, it is our duty at once to interpose.' And British forces in the region remained adequately prepared for such a contingency.[3]

Although British representatives in the Gulf attempted to refrain from meddling in internal issues they carefully followed local events. In May 1883, the Political Resident's diary had recorded animosity between the Shaikhs of Abu Dhabi and Dubai. As a result, the Shaikh of Dubai had taken precautions and entered into a defensive alliance with the chief of Sharjah.[4] Six years later, however, the Shaikh of Abu Dhabi, Shaikh Zaid bin Khalifa, and the Shaikh of Dubai, Shaikh Rashid bin Maktum, made an agreement to coordinate their forces against the Shaikh of Qatar, Shaikh Jasim bin Thani. According to the British Political Agent in Sharjah, the rulers of Abu Dhabi and Dubai were enraged by the behavior of Shaikh Jasim. Reporting from Sharjah, the Political Agent explained that during an attack on a neighboring territory Shaikh Jasim had ordered his men to kill women and children. Members of his Bedouin force protested that 'no Arab had ever done such a thing as kill women and children, but Jasim did not listen to them.'[5]

Shaikh Jasim bin Mohammed Al Thani, who had infuriated his neighbors, considered it prudent to justify his conduct. Writing to the Political Resident, he noted that his own son had earlier been killed by his enemies and expressed the wish that he would have additional opportunity for revenge. Shaikh Jasim declared, 'I have hope in God and in you that you will not countenance the intention of the oppressors, and I hope that your subjects and agents in Oman may refrain from interference in that which does not concern them.'[6]

As conflict among shaikhs continued, in May 1889, the government of India acknowledged that it was important to halt the spread of violence and suggested that Her Majesty's Government (HMG) attempt to take effective steps to do so.[7] British efforts were not always successful and sometimes the shaikhs themselves resolved their difficulties. In March 1894, the British Political Resident's diary noted that the chief of Abu Dhabi had arranged reconciliation between the Shaikhs of Sharjah and Dubai.[8] Two months later, after an outbreak of hostilities between two tribes in his territories, the Hinawis and Ghafiris, the Sultan of Muscat and Oman brought their leaders together and arranged a settlement.[9] Oman was not officially a British protected state, and had diplomatic relations with foreign powers, including the United States. Nevertheless, at the beginning of June, after a quarrel between the contending groups resulted in a riot on the beach at Matrah, the Sultan sent his *Wazir* to request British advice on how to deal with the conflict.[10]

The Gulf rulers' relationship with Britain served further to enhance their status.

The one important and constant element in the political evolution of the Gulf states was the position of the ruler. He signed the treaties, and he was personally responsible for the application of all their clauses. The British authorities – whether the Political Resident, the Political Agent or the Senior Naval Officer of the Persian Gulf Division – dealt with him alone. The treaty system strengthened his position and assured the continuity of his influence. With time, it became a guarantee. Most important, it contributed to the institutionalization of his position.[11]

Thus, as the twentieth century began, HMG continued to act as guardian of the Gulf and adviser to its rulers. In 1903, after both Russian and French warships visited the Gulf, accompanied by a fleet of six British men-of-war and two Indian marine vessels, the Viceroy of India Lord Curzon of Kedleston arrived for a tour. Lord Curzon, who traveled on the cruiser *Argonaut*, the largest ship heretofore to enter Arab Gulf waters, had earlier proclaimed that any Englishman who allowed a foreign nation to infiltrate the Gulf was a traitor.[12]

With the discovery of oil the region assumed additional importance. Hence, the loss of empire after World War II did not diminish Britain's interest. In 1946, the British Residency was transferred from Bushire on the Iranian coast to Bahrain on the Arab side of the Gulf. Through Political Agents responsible to him, the Political Resident continued to maintain close contact with the rulers of Bahrain, Qatar, Kuwait, the Trucial States, and Oman. Excluding Oman these shaikhdoms were small in both size and population. As yet, no steps had been taken 'to release the shaykhdoms from the fragmented isolation in which, as in aspic, the treaties preserved them.'[13]

Gradually, however, oil revenue, which went directly to the Gulf State treasuries, provided the means to develop the region. Enormous resources led to a rapid change in the lives of the inhabitants, who replaced their camels with automobiles, and established modern shopping malls stocked with an abundance of imported luxury goods. 'The most distinctive political aspect of the Arab monarchies of the Gulf is that the governments have access to enormous wealth, particularly in light of their relatively small population, without having to tax their societies.'[14]

As Gulf citizens began to enjoy the blessings of abundance, guest workers, soon to outnumber the original inhabitants, provided labor. Africans and Asians, including Egyptians, Palestinians, Yemenites, Iraqis, Filipinos, Indians and Pakistanis arrived in the protected shaikhdoms. Unskilled foreign workers built schools, homes, hospitals, and roads. They planted trees, cleaned the streets, and served as household helpers. Educated foreign employees found employment as teachers, managers, and administrators. As the wealth of the region increased, each ruler, as paramount shaikh of all of his territory's tribes, continued to meet with the traditional tribal council. Now these meetings 'rarely occur in tents, but usually in air-conditioned palaces, and are recorded so that clips can be shown on evening television news programs.'[15]

During the 1950s, impressed with Egyptian leader Abdul Gamal Nasser, foreign Arab workers carried Arab nationalism into the developing Gulf region. According to Conservative Prime Minister Harold Macmillan:

> Wherever one looked in the Middle East there were traces of Nasser's baneful operations. Against all this we could only strive to maintain our traditional spheres of influence. We fully realised the vital importance of the Gulf and of Aden.[16]

In 1956, Britain's unsuccessful attempt to reoccupy the Suez Canal and to topple Egyptian leader Nasser resulted in displays of anti-British sentiment in the shaikhdoms, but did not alienate Gulf rulers. However, the Suez episode underlined both Britain's loss of power and the growing strength of Arab nationalism. London was dismayed when Washington demanded that Britain, together with her allies France and Israel, quickly withdraw from Egyptian soil. Writing in his diary on 5 December 1956, British Foreign Official Evelyn Shuckburgh lamented:

> Now that our withdrawal 'without delay' from Suez has been announced by Selwyn Lloyd everyone at the IDC [Imperial Defence College] has become suddenly very gloomy and all the services feel they have been betrayed, and we will never be able to show any independence as a nation again.[17]

Clearly Britain had lost prestige. Egypt now encouraged Arabs throughout the Middle East to disregard their own leaders and to turn to Nasser. Motivated by self-preservation, the Gulf shaikhs ignored Britain's reduced standing and continued to look to HMG for protection. At the same time, Gulf rulers considered how to join forces. Writing in 1963, historian Elizabeth Monroe speculated:

> In the bottom of most hearts in the Gulf sheikhdoms, there is a hankering ultimately to belong to some larger unit than a principality that is in some cases little more than a family estate, or an oilfield.[18]

During the 1960s, Gulf ruling families wanted British officials to assist in resolving quarrels among themselves and also to prepare a framework for unification. Moreover, throughout the 1960s, not only were Gulf shaikhs uncomfortable with Nasser, they were aware of potential threats from their powerful and sometimes difficult Muslim neighbors, Saudi Arabia, Iraq and Iran. Thus, throughout the 1960s as in previous years, the British tried to assist the Gulf States to settle disputes among themselves and with their larger neighbors. British attention helped resolve several territorial issues, including the long dispute between Bahrain and Qatar over title to the village of Zubara, which was located on the Qatar peninsula.[19]

Yet, as it turned out, the 1960s were to be Britain's last complete decade in the Gulf. In October 1964, the Labour Party, led by Harold Wilson, won a majority in the House of Commons. The new Chancellor of the Exchequer, James Callaghan, was distressed to learn that Britain had a huge £800 million balance of payment deficit. Opposing devaluation, Labour preferred to cut defense spending. As a result, the government considered how to reduce defense commitments.[20] Yet, despite the emotional crisis that resulted from Israel's victory in the June 1967 Six-Day War, neither Gulf rulers nor their subjects demanded that Britain go.

During the 1960s, as development proceeded at a rapid pace, the British government did its utmost to provide guidance to Gulf shaikhs. At the beginning of what was to be their final years as guardians of the Gulf, British officials pressed for political progress, cooperation among the shaikhdoms and improvements in education and healthcare. At the same time, of course, Foreign Office officials continued to safeguard specific British economic interests and the political interests of the western alliance.

NOTES

1. J.B. Kelly, *Britain and the Persian Gulf, 1795–1880* (Oxford: Oxford University Press, 1968), pp. 50–2.
2. Hussain Albaharna, *The Legal Status of the Arabian Gulf States* (Manchester: Manchester University Press, 1968), p. 5.
3. Letter, No. 226, Jones to Ethersey, Bushire, Residency Records, Persian Gulf, Bushire, Pt 1, R/15/1/157, British Library.
4. Political Diary, R/15/1/193, Bushire, 25 May 1883, British Library.
5. Letter, Political Agent to Political Resident, Sharjah, 19 February 1889, Residency records, Persian Gulf, Bushire, 1880–1890, Pt 2, R/15/1/189, British Library.

6.   Letter, Political Agent to Political Resident, Sharjah, 8 March 1889, Residency Records, Persian Gulf, Bushire, 1880–1890, Pt 2, R/15/1/189, British Library.
7.   Letter, No. 74, Governor of India Foreign Department to Cross, Simla, 24 May 1889, Residency Records, Persian Gulf, Bushire, 1880–1890, Pt 2, British Library.
8.   Political Diary, R/15/1/194, Sharjah, 22 March 1894, British Library.
9.   Political Diary, R/15/1/194, Muscat, 11 May 1894, British Library.
10. Political Diary, R/15/1/194, Muscat, 4 June 1894, British Library.
11. Rosemaries Said Zahlan, *The Making of the Modern Gulf States* (Reading, MA: Ithaca, 1998), p. 27.
12. Miriam Joyce, *The Sultanate of Oman: A Twentieth Century History* (Westport, CT: Praeger, 1995). p. 7.
13. Glen Balfour-Paul, *The End of Empire in the Middle East* (Cambridge, Cambridge University Press, 1994), p. 103.
14. F. Gregory Gause III, *Oil Monarchies* (New York: Council on Foreign Relations, 1994) p. 42.
15. F. Gregory Gause III, *Oil Monarchies* (New York: Council on Foreign Relations, 1994) p. 25.
16. Harold Macmillan, *Pointing the Way* (New York: Harper & Row, 1972), p. 382.
17. Evelyn Shuckburgh, *Descent to Suez* (New York: Norton, 1987), p. 366.
18. Elizabeth Monroe, *Britain's Moment in the Middle East: 1914–1956* (Baltimore, MD: Johns Hopkins University Press, 1963), pp. 216–17.
19. Glen Balfour-Paul, *The End of Empire in the Middle East* (Cambridge, Cambridge University Press, 1994), p. 113.
20. Frank Brenchley, *Britain and the Middle East: An Economic History 1945–87* (London: Lester Crook, 1989), pp. 165–6.

1

The Trucial States

As the decade of the 1960s began, the seven shaikhdoms, known as the Trucial States, Abu Dhabi, Dubai, Sharjah, Ajman, Umm Al Qawain, Ras Al Khaimah, and Fujairah, an area of 32,000 square miles, remained dependent on Britain for protection and economic assistance. There were numerous differences among the rulers and sometimes quarrels between members of the same ruling family. Her Majesty's Government (HMG) wished to retain its position in the region, but at the same time wanted the various ruling shaikhs to work together to ensure stability and to improve conditions for the area's inhabitants.

In order to enhance cooperation among the seven Trucial rulers, in 1952, Britain had established a Trucial State Council, but at the beginning of the 1960s, British officials hesitated to call a meeting of that Council, which had not met in two years. It appeared that one of the most important rulers, Abu Dhabi's Shaikh Shakhbut bin Sultan Al Nuhayyan, was unlikely to attend. Abu Dhabi's ruler was at loggerheads with Britain over two issues: a long-standing dispute with neighboring Qatar and legal jurisdiction in his shaikhdom. Shaikh Shakhbut claimed a portion of coast that extended up to Umm Said and some small islands off the Qatar peninsula, including the island of Halul. In addition, Shaikh Shakhbut wanted the British to surrender court jurisdiction in his state. Prior to relinquishing jurisdiction London insisted that Abu Dhabi modernize its legal system.

Although British officials considered Shaikh Shakhbut difficult and unpredictable, Assistant Head of Whitehall's Arabian Department Robert Walmsley was confident that the ruler of Abu Dhabi was 'a gentleman' and, therefore, a satisfactory formula could be worked out.[1] London told Shaikh Shakhbut that it was ready to follow the same process that earlier had been applied to Kuwait; a step-by-step procedure with the British turning over legal jurisdiction after adequate local legislation was in place. To start the process, London was willing to permit Shaikh Shakhbut jurisdiction over all Muslims except Turks, and Pakistanis. The ruler was not satisfied.[2]

Although Shaikh Shakhbut was receiving income from Trucial States Petroleum Development Ltd, and Abu Dhabi Marine Areas Ltd (ADMA), companies developing oilfields in his shaikhdom, he spent little on public improvement. British officials speculated that Shaikh Shakhbut had accumulated approximately £1 million, which he put in five-gallon oil tins and placed under his bed. Although he had agreed to donate 4 percent of his income toward the economic development of the entire area, Shaikh Shakhbut had not done so. Hence, he was unpopular with his subjects and with the other shaikhdoms.[3]

Therefore, despite the presence of oil companies there were few significant signs of change in Abu Dhabi. ADMA's presence, however, provided what became a popular form of evening entertainment. The company set up a projector near the beach. Using the wall of a house, ADMA showed movies to a delighted audience, which sat on the sand. Recalling his childhood in Abu Dhabi, Mohammed Al Fahim wrote:

> We loved to see the cowboys in their strange hats, riding horses and firing from their six-shooters. Sometimes, much to our delight and amazement, they would show a cartoon before the film started. We were captivated by the animated characters and their crazy antics.[4]

Meanwhile, interested in enhancing Britain's reputation in the Trucial States, Political Resident Sir George Middleton wished to give each of the seven rulers a new saluting gun. The saluting guns in use were 'antique and dangerous to their friends.'[5] Whitehall doubted that the Treasury would approve because 'the idea of just gratifying the whims of autocrats in matters which do not benefit subjects in the slightest provides fair game for parliamentary criticism.'[6]

Since London resisted, Sir George reduced his request, asking only for guns to present to the rulers of Ajman and Umm al Qawain. When the Foreign Office continued to have difficulty convincing the Treasury, Political Resident Middleton argued that he was not suggesting Britain 'gratify the whims of autocrats.' The rulers were in charge because it had long been British policy to protect them.

> The more we can get them on our side, the easier it will be to guide these Rulers along the right path in their affairs for the betterment of their people. In other words a little gun can go a long way in helping us in our policies here. It is vital that we should retain the good will of the Trucial Shaikhs and I think the expenditure of just over £500 on these 'toys' for the two Rulers will be well worth while.[7]

Finally, in July 1960, the Foreign Office ordered the purchase of two 25-pound guns. Afterwards, these guns were shipped to Aden. The War Office requested that, once the guns arrived there, local officials arrange transportation to Ajman and Umm Al Qawain.[8]

Now British attention turned to Dubai, where the shaikhdom's port continued to grow and to earn income from customs duties. In 1957, a Municipal Council had been formed and, together with the ruler Shaikh Rashid bin Said Al Maktum, began an extensive planning program. Three years later, Dubai Creek was dredged to permit seven- foot draft vessels to cross the bar at all times. A new airport was opened, a modern telephone system installed, and work on electrical and water supply facilities was in progress.[9]

Smuggling, however, remained an important economic activity. Gold was freely imported into the shaikhdom and then, 'with the connivance of poorly paid' customs officials, transported in motorized dhows into India and Pakistan. Visiting Dubai at the beginning of December 1961, American Consul in Dhahran John E. Horner called at the office of Shaikh Rashid Al Maktum who referred to his city as 'the Venice of the East.' Horner noted that, unlike the other rulers of the region, Shaikh Rashid did not receive him in the usual *majlis* (meeting room), but in a small office furnished with a steel desk. From his office, Shaikh Rashid actively promoted the development of his territory and opportunity for his 45,000 subjects.[10] On a later visit, however, Horner commented on the absence of education in the shaikhdom. At the end of June 1962, the American official was surprised to see a life preserver with Hebrew letters attached to the stern of a dhow which was anchored alongside Dubai Creek harbor. The life preserver had been found at sea and picked up as salvage without any understanding of its Israeli connection. According to Horner, the incident had no political significance, but illustrated the ignorance that prevailed in even the most advanced Trucial State.[11]

Arriving in Dubai four years later, the newly appointed Political Agent, D.A. Roberts, was amazed at the variety of commercial activities in progress. Like Consul General Horner, Roberts was impressed by the energy and ability of Shaikh Rashid, who had created a modern town before he had the benefit of oil wealth.

> It requires a conscious and continuous effort not to be captivated by Sheikh Rashid's devastating charm, with which goes an agile brain, simplicity of personal life, generosity, and an immense capacity for hard work. One has to remind oneself continually how devious he is and how ruthless he is capable of being when he sees his objective clearly.[12]

Neighboring Sharjah did not have Dubai's advantages. Sharjah suffered from the absence of an adequate water supply and in the summer of 1960, with the exception of a few private generators, there was no electricity available in the state. The only hospital in the Sharjah, the American Mission Hospital, was 'desperately over-worked.' The one doctor, Sarah Hosman, was 84 years old. She administered to so many patients that babies were delivered outside the hospital in the street or in cars. The ruler offered to provide additional space, but his offer did not resolve the problem of staffing.[13]

As HMG wrestled with the difficulties of how to maintain stability and at the same time to promote development, the United States began to show an increased interest in the Trucial States. Prior to relinquishing his post in Saudi Arabia, in January 1961 American Consul General in Dhahran Walter K. Schwinn visited all of the Trucial States with the exception of Fujairah. Schwinn reported to Washington that the rulers were genuinely pleased that an official representative of the United States had called. The shaikhs expressed considerable interest in the new American administration. 'Virtually all, after inquiring of the health of the President asked God to give him strength and success.' As a result of his visits Schwinn recommended that annual calls be paid to the Trucial State rulers.[14]

During his farewell tour, the American Consul General asked Political Agent in Dubai Donald Hawley for his opinion about the possibility of forging a federation of the Trucial States. Hawley was skeptical that federation was possible. He predicted that Abu Dhabi's Shaikh Shakhbut would soon have a large income from the oil resources of his territory and would, therefore, be unwilling to cooperate. Hawley claimed that the other rulers would not oppose Shaikh Shakhbut 'either through fear of his wrath or desire for his favor.' Nevertheless, Hawley was not prepared to proceed with a plan for a federation that did not include Abu Dhabi; a plan which would form a union of the six other Trucial States with Dubai in a leading role. The American blamed Britain for contributing to the difficulty in establishing a union of all seven states. Schwinn said that earlier, Britain should have decisively acted to create a federation, 'even at the cost of arm-twisting.' According to the American Consul General:

> As matters now stand, federation of all the Trucial States seems likely to remain an iridescent dream or, at best, a truncated and ineffectual affair subject to constant intrigue and plotting.[15]

In April 1961, all seven rulers attended the sixteenth meeting of the Trucial Council, which was held in Dubai. During the meeting, Political Agent Hawley, who served as chairman, announced that Britain planned to spend more than £800,000 on development in the next five years.[16] Funds would be available for public health, agricultural stations and education, including sending Trucial State subjects abroad to study. Later, in his farewell address, the departing Political Resident Sir George Middleton emphasized the importance of collaboration among the states:

> There is an Arabic Proverb which says that 'one's neighbour matters more than one's house, and one's travelling companion more than the road on which one travels.' We are all neighbours now. The rapid improvements in communications have made us so. Increasing cooperation is therefore essential for the future development and welfare of the Trucial States...[17]

After the meeting, Hawley reiterated his opinion that prospects for a federation uniting the Trucial States were not good as long as the ruler of Abu Dhabi continued to participate in the Council.[18]

During the summer of 1961, Shaikh Shakhbut finally invited several large contractors to visit his state to discuss development possibilities. He made some agreements, but abruptly changed his mind and dismissed the visiting businessmen. Given Shaikh Shakhbut's temperament, several companies decided that the best way to approach him was first to become established in the region and earn a good reputation. A few had earlier been successful. After establishing a bank branch in Sharjah, the Eastern Bank was permitted to open one in Abu Dhabi, and following its success in Dubai, the British Bank of the Middle East was also allowed to open in Shaikh Shakhbut's territory.[19]

Relations between the British and Shaikh Shakhbut, however, continued to be strained. In March 1962, the British awarded the disputed island of Halul to the Shaikh of Qatar.[20] Shaikh Shakhbut was disappointed and angry. Political Agent Colonel Hugh Boustead pointed out that Abu Dhabi had failed to provide evidence to the arbitration commission and that perhaps if the shaikhdom had done so Halul would have been awarded to Shaikh Shakhbut.[21]

Foreign Office officials patiently pursued efforts to influence Abu Dhabi's ruler to develop his territory. Finally, Shaikh Shakhbut agreed to appoint experts to approve development projects. It also appeared that the ruler agreed to separate his personal funds from state funds.

In May 1961, Sir William Luce was promoted to what was now the most senior British appointment in the Arab world, Political Resident in the Persian Gulf. The new Political Resident suggested that Shaikh Shakhbut take 20 percent of the shaikhdom's revenue for his personal use and permit the state to utilize the remaining 80 percent. American observers were not optimistic that such a division would be implemented.[22]

By spring 1962 there was some evidence of development in Abu Dhabi, with construction of the small Emile Bustani Hotel in progress and two new unpaved roads. However, given the oil wealth now available so much more could have been accomplished. Always reluctant to spend money, Shaikh Shakhbut awaited the results of a town plan being prepared by Political Agent Hugh Boustead. Meanwhile, the ruler continued to limit the number of merchants, including those from neighboring Dubai, permitted to enter his shaikhdom even to establish partnerships with his subjects.[23]

Finally, in the summer of 1963, Shaikh Shakhbut appeared willing to move forward. He signed a £5 million plan for development; a plan that included construction of an airport, a 70 kilometer water pipeline and two new schools. The British were delighted. Her Majesty's officials claimed that 'their miserly shaykh' had been frightened into spending money by a recent wave of strikes in the oil fields.[24]

Profits from Trucial State oil now appeared certain. Therefore, London did not want to increase the £100,000 per annum that the British government devoted to Trucial Coast development. Kuwait expressed willing to step in and provide grants.[25] However, the amirate did not want to contribute to the common development fund, but to individual rulers. American observers suggested that perhaps Kuwait's government was motivated by a desire to reduce British control over how funds would be spent and also to discourage cooperation among the Trucial shaikhs.[26]

Meanwhile, in Ras Al Khaimah under the shaikhdom's one-eyed ruler, Shaikh Saqr bin Mohammed Al Qasimi, there were signs of progress. The British had sponsored an experimental farm with approximately one thousand irrigation pumps, which served as a model for the region, and Shaikh Saqr encouraged his subjects to benefit from the facility. As the agricultural experimental station continued to achieve positive results its director, Theodore Morgan, indicated that it was possible to grow vegetables in the shaikhdom. Morgan claimed that while the high salinity of the water supply caused some difficulties, these problems could be resolved. The station provided local farmers with seeds, advised them on methods, and assisted in marketing their produce. The British speculated that local products would become so abundant that the Trucial States would no longer need to import fruits and vegetables from India and Pakistan.[27]

Foreign observers praised Shaikh Saqr bin Mohammed for doing more to assist his people than any other Trucial State ruler except Dubai's Shaikh Rashid.[28] The British were especially pleased that Shaikh Saqr bin Mohammed claimed that the division of the Trucial Coast into seven small states was 'absurd' and that, therefore, he steadfastly advocated union.[29] The intelligent and thoughtful ruler of Ras Al Khaimah faced serious problems. The sea was eroding his town; he suspected one of his brothers of plotting against him; he had constantly to guard against possible eruption of conflict with several tribes, including the Khawatir, the Harbus and 'the wild Highland men of the Shihuh'.[30]

Given his problems, Shaikh Saqr bin Mohammed Al Qasimi was not convinced that the British did enough to support him. Hence, he sought American assistance. While serving as an attaché at the American Embassy in Kuwait, Robert E. Rice attended Kuwait's Independence Day celebrations. During the festivities the American was introduced to Shaikh Saqr's brother. After Rice expressed an interest in Ras Al Khaimah he received an invitation to visit and the British issued a visa. Although initially reluctant to travel during the hot summer months, Rice agreed to do so. On 2 August, the American left for Ras Al Khaimah accompanied by an Iraqi businessman, Abdul Amir Al Ghazi. Shaikh Saqr bin Mohammed told his guest that British development assistance was insufficient and that he preferred that American rather than British firms should exploit possible oil resources in his territory.[31]

Although HMG accepted that American economic competition was inevitable, Britian was not yet prepared to relinquish her dominance in the Gulf. In January 1963, during discussions with American Consul General Horner, Political Resident Sir William declared that access to Gulf oil was essential to Europe. It was necessary to maintain stability in the regime and to contain Egyptian leader Abdul Gamal Nasser. Sir William hoped that Washington understood the need for Britain to remain in the Gulf for the 'indefinite future.' The Political Resident also considered it 'absolutely essential' that London and Washington followed a common policy in the region.[32] American officials in the Gulf wholeheartedly agreed. According to Consul General Horner:

As seen from here, it is clearly in U.S. interests that U.K. maintain its special relationship with Gulf shaykhdoms, and retain its military forces in area, hopefully long enough for shaykhdoms to acquire minimum competence to assume control of their own affairs.[33]

Of course, American companies continued to pursue economic opportunities in the Gulf. As a result of an invitation issued in the summer of 1963 by the Mecom organization, which had oil concessions in several Trucial States, Sharjah's ruler, Saqr bin Sultan Al Qasimi, visited Washington. A Mecom employee, W. Angie Smith, asked the American Ambassador in Jordan, William B. Macomber Jr, to inform the State Department about Shaikh Saqr bin Sultan's upcoming visit. Although the ruler of Sharjah did not expect any particular attention, the British Ambassador in Washington was planning a luncheon and hoped that some arrangement might be made for Shaikh Saqr bin Sultan to call at the State Department.[34] When Sharjah's ruler arrived in Washington, Dubai's ruler, Shaikh Rashid, was also visiting. As a result, the State Department hosted a luncheon for each of the Rulers. According to their American hosts, Shaikh Rashid made an excellent impression, but Shaikh Saqr appeared 'ill at ease in the unfamiliar surroundings.'[35]

During his trip to the United States, Sharjah's Shaikh Saqr bin Sultan visited Houston where he graciously answered 'endless indelicate' questions about polygamous family life, patiently posed for pictures in a cowboy hat and received the key to the city from the mayor. Responding to questions about what he would do with the revenue when oil was found in his territory, Sharjah's ruler stated that wealth resulting from oil would not belong to him, but to his people. Such wealth would be used to improve education, healthcare and agriculture. Speaking privately to the British Consul General in Houston, the ruler expressed his distaste for skyscrapers and 'the bustle of contemporary American life.'[36]

Traveling Trucial State rulers also visited London during the summer of 1963. Both Shaikh Rashid of Dubai and Shaikh Ahmad bin Rashid Al Mu'alla of Umm al Qawain had earlier expressed a wish to meet the Queen. Not every Trucial State ruler was given that privilege. The ruler of Umm al Qawain was considered wise, straight-forward and a competent administrator, but Shaikh Ahmad's state was poor. He earned most of his revenue from the taxi service he ran between Dubai, Sharjah, Umm al Qawain and the Batinah coast. 'There could be no question of arranging an Audience for so minor a

Ruler.' For whatever arrangements were made for one of the least important Trucial State rulers would in future have to be made for all the others.[37] The Foreign Office asked the Lord Chamberlain to arrange that, at a garden party, the two Gulf rulers, Rashid of Dubai and Ahmad of Umm al Qawain, 'be placed strategically in a lane and subsequently to take tea in the Royal tent.'[38] Arrangements were made and each shaikh, accompanied by one of his sons, attended a Royal garden party where he met the Queen and Prince Philip.[39] The visit of the two rulers was a success. An official in the Lord Chamberlain's Office wrote to a Foreign Office colleague that perhaps the happy shaikhs would provide 'you and I an oil-well between us.'[40]

While in London, Shaikh Rashid bin Said Al Maktum was concerned with issues other than garden parties. He was unhappy with the frontier between Sharjah and Abu Dhabi. Claiming that in 1948 British officials had established an unfair boundary, he requested an adjustment.[41] But Shaikh Rashid did not want such issues to stand in the way of a future federation of Trucial States. He envisioned establishment of joint departments to control ports, immigration and police. He also advocated establishment of a high court composed of representatives of all seven rulers accompanied by their chosen legal advisers.[42] While in London, Dubai's ruler arranged to conduct business with private commercial firms, 'somewhat to the disgust of the Political Agent who considers that such money grubbing demeans the Ruler's personal dignity and the prestige of his office.' American Consul General Horner disagreed with the Political Agent. Shaikh Rashid was a businessman and 'may well feel he should not eschew any good opportunity.'[43]

During the summer of 1963, British attention also focused on festivities that took place in the Gulf when Shaikh Shakhbut's son, Said bin Shakhbut Al Nuhayyan, married his first cousin, daughter of Shaikh Zaid bin Sultan Al Nuhayyan, which took place in Buraimi. Hundreds of guests from neighboring states attended the celebration. Despite the intense heat, dancing continued day and night. Camel and horse races occupied the guests who were also entertained by pipes and drums. All sorts of guns, including modern sub-machine guns, were fired 'and enough ammunition was expended to fight a medium sized battle.' During the dancing, a guest accidentally fired his machine gun, seriously wounding three others. 'Even this, however, did not appear to upset the festivities unduly.' A British participant speculated that the wedding might be the last such affair in Abu Dhabi:

> The first advance guards of the 20th century were already visible in the fleets of American cars, in the neon lights at the night dances and in the fact that some of the singers and musicians were recording themselves on tape recorders; I suppose we must resign ourselves to the prospect that in a few years' time, weddings in Abu Dhabi may be celebrated by drinking Pepsi Cola and dancing the Twist.[44]

Despite the wedding celebration, Shaikh Shakhbut was not entirely happy. He was disturbed about negative publicity he had received in the western press. In August, American Consul James A. May visited Abu Dhabi and afterwards sent a brief note to the ruler thanking him for his warm hospitality.[45] Shaikh Shakhbut responded with a long letter asking May to visit frequently. Complaining bitterly about recent press reports that had been published about him in the United States, Shaikh Shakhbut asked May to inform the 'owners of your newspapers' that they were mistaken about Shaikh Shakhbut.[46] Embarrassed that the Ruler of a British protected state had addressed such a letter to an American official, May provided the Political Residency in Bahrain with copies of his correspondence.[47] According to the British Foreign Office, the Americans in Dhahran 'will think twice about sending even innocuous letters to Shakhbut in future.'[48]

Political Agent Duncan Slater also visited Shaikh Shakhbut during the summer of 1963. When the ruler complained about the bad press he had received in both Britain and the United States, Slater told him that criticism was the 'inevitable price of fame,' that it was unjust to blame certain firms for critical articles. Slater reminded the ruler that the British press was free and that the government could not control publications. Slater advised that the best way to avoid criticism was to spend his income to develop his country.[49] Shaikh Shakhbut would not leave the issue. He insisted that foreign firms in Abu Dhabi influence newspaper publishers at home to print complimentary articles about him. Commenting on Shaikh Shakhbut's demand, a Whitehall official remarked that the ruler 'is being unscrupulous and at the same time naive.'[50]

Wishing to conduct business in Abu Dhabi, the Eastern Bank attempted to please the ruler by securing the favorable publicity he desired. The British press refused entreaties to publish complimentary articles. Hence, with authorization to pay up to £2,000, the bank's management turned to the Lebanese press. According to an official at the British Embassy in Beirut, 'one could obtain good publicity for almost any cause in any Lebanese paper provided one was prepared to pay for it.'[51]

Iran now began to express an increased interest in the Gulf shaikhdoms. In Tehran, both the Prime Minister and Foreign Minister told British Ambassador Sir Dennis Wright that the Shah's government was prepared to play an expanded role in the region. They suggested that Persian language and culture be used to counter Nasser's influence. In addition, Iranian officials speculated about the possibility of Iran's becoming 'the honest broker' between London and the Gulf rulers. Sir Dennis reminded the Iranians that Britain alone was responsible for the foreign relations of the shaikhdoms and emphasized that HMG did not require any assistance.[52] American Consul General Horner approved of the British position. He continued to claim that Washington's interests would best be served if Britain maintained its special relationship with the Trucial States and that it was important for the British to retain their military forces in the Gulf until the shaikhdoms acquired the competence to take charge of their own affairs.[53]

Meanwhile, the Trucial States Council scheduled its eighteenth session for 13 January 1964. On the agenda was a proposal to establish a joint court to hear cases in which the parties involved in a dispute came from different shaikhdoms. Among other items to be discussed was the possibility of a toll for cars using certain roads, including the road through the Wadi Ham to Fujairah and Khorfakkan. Also on the agenda was the establishment of a Deliberative Committee of delegates from each state to work out details of various proposals and look into coordination of education and improvement of health facilities.[54]

Shaikh Shakhbut, who had been absent during the previous three years, attended the January 1964 meeting. However, Abu Dhabi's ruler arrived two hours late and then refused to commit himself on any issue, except to agree to a United Nations Desert Locust Operational Research Aerial Unit. Shaikh Rashid, too, appeared to lack enthusiasm for the agenda. Political Agent Craig reported to Political Resident Luce:

> The Rulers are naturally reactionary in deed, even though one or the other may occasionally permit himself the luxury of a progressive outburst. In the face of this attitude we shall have to press central institutions upon them. This will mean, I fear, that we shall have to make it a point of our policy to give active support to those economic and social factors which will increasingly lead to the dominance of one or two centres of power.[55]

Foreign Office official Frank Brenchley suggested that only the apportionment of Abu Dhabi's oil wealth would give the other rulers enough incentive to combine their interests. Brenchley advised that British officials 'sell' Shaikh Shakhbut on the wisdom of sharing.[56]

Writing to the Political Agent in Dubai at the end of January 1964, Political Resident Luce stated that HMG would remain in the Gulf 'until some valid alternative to the Pax Britannica emerges.' Hence, it was essential that Her Majesty's officials do everything possible 'to improve the public appearance of the relationship between ourselves and the Gulf States.' Working towards the unity of the Trucial States was a priority. According to Sir William:

> We have no hope of convincing anyone, not even ourselves, that the individual States, particularly Fujairah, Ajman and Um al Qawain, are anything more than puppets, totally dependent on our support for their survival. But a federation of these States, though still small and weak, could just be viable and would certainly be internationally more respectable.[57]

Efforts to unify the Trucial States continued. In March 1964, the Political Resident told the Foreign Office that although it might sometimes be difficult to arrange interesting agendas he anticipated that the Trucial States Council would meet four times a year.[58] In what areas was cooperation feasible? A Trucial State roads department was a good idea, but there were no available funds to spend on roads. A Trucial State education department appeared sensible, but funds for schools came from a variety of sources unlikely to cooperate. A Trucial State passport would be a sign of unity, but each ruler zealously guarded his right to issue his own passports.[59] Sale of passports provided income that was especially needed by the poorer rulers who granted passports valid for only a year or two. Rulers also gained revenue from the sale of stamps. Income from the 'stamp-dealing racket' was substantial. As a result, it was difficult to convince the rulers to establish a common postal service.[60]

Abu Dhabi remained the key to organizing a federation of these states, but the British were concerned that 'Shakhbut would not play.'[61] In June 1964, all of the Trucial State rulers attended the nineteenth session of the Trucial State Council. Reports on Trucial States development activities were the main focus of the meeting. The rulers appeared most interested in the reports on agriculture. When the issue of passports was discussed, only the ruler of Ras Al Khaimah favored the idea of a single Trucial State passport. The establishment of a joint immigrant department was also on the agenda, but here too it was impossible to achieve consensus. Political Agent Craig spoke to the assembled rulers and expressed concern about their failure to cooperate with each other.

> The Rulers were certainly embarrassed: but it was an embarrassment which disappeared with the announcement shortly afterwards that lunch was ready. I am more than ever convinced that federation or cooperation (it is better at this stage to avoid the former word, which I suspect, frightens some of the Rulers) will only come through the introduction of specific and limited schemes in specific and limited spheres.[62]

Although moving the Trucial States toward cooperation was a difficult task, Political Resident Luce assured Craig that it was essential to continue pressing.[63]

At the end of 1964, the United States wished to open a branch consular office in Dubai. Deputy Director for Near East Affairs at the State Department, Harrison Symmes, told British official Patrick Wright that Washington had received several reports which indicated that the Arab League planned an office in Dubai. Wright denied that this was the case. However, Symmes did not appear convinced and declared that, since it was impossible to predict how the rulers would react to requests for foreign consular representation after the British transfer of jurisdiction took place, it would now be prudent to admit American representation. Although the State Department was in the midst of efforts to cut costs and, hence, close some consular posts, Washington attached considerable importance to opening a Trucial State consulate. Symmes reported to London that the State Department was willing to accept a British proposal that instead of opening a consulate, Washington establish a trade mission. Nevertheless, this solution would not meet American requirements unless the trade agent was empowered to act as a consul and authenticate documents. Earlier, the Foreign Office had proposed that the American Consul in Dhahran conduct consular affairs in the Trucial Coast. Wright repeated this proposal, but Symmes demurred, pointing out that the distance between Dhahran and the Trucial States made such an arrangement inconvenient.[64]

London remained unwilling to encourage an official American presence but continued to promote a closer relationship among the small states of the region. In December 1964, the brother of the ruler of Bahrain, Shaikh Khalifa bin Sulman Al Khalifa, visited Abu Dhabi;

his first visit to any of the Trucial States. Shaikh Shakhbut agreed that it was wise for the Trucial States and Bahrain to work together. United in their suspicion of Nasser and the Arab League, Shaikhs Khalifa and Shakhbut decided to seek cooperation with Saudi Arabia. They also discussed a common currency. Shaikh Khalifa claimed that Bahrain would be willing to join the Trucial States in establishing such a currency, and that it was likely Qatar, too, would join. However, he suggested that Bahrain be the location of the Central Currency Board.[65]

Among British concerns at the beginning of 1965 was growing Egyptian influence in Sharjah, which was encouraged by Shaikh Saqr bin Sultan Al Qasimi. Political Resident Luce authorized Political Agent Glen Balfour-Paul to pin the ruler 'politically to the wall.' Balfour-Paul told Shaikh Saqr bin Sultan that London objected to his close involvement with the United Arab Republic (UAR). Either he had inadvertently become 'the plaything of the Egyptians' or he had willingly joined Cairo despite Nasser's intention to use the Arab League to create chaos in the region and destroy shaikhly rule. Shaikh Saqr bin Sultan assured Balfour-Paul that he did not want to become a victim of Arab socialism, 'wandering the world as a penniless exile.' At the same time, Sharjah's ruler insisted that Britain try to understand his situation. He had no money to develop his state and Egypt was the only country to offer him the assistance he required. Yet he was afraid of Egypt, and his expressions of 'Arab nationalist zeal were largely dictated by fear.'[66]

Committed to limiting Arab League activity in the Gulf, Political Resident Sir William visited the six northern rulers in the middle of February 1965. He warned that a planned Arab League Development Office in their region would result in grave danger to the shaikhdoms. He urged that during the next meeting of the Trucial States Council they pass a resolution establishing their own Development Office.[67] Disregarding the Political Resident's warning, when the twenty-first session of the Trucial States Council met on 1 March the rulers appeared unwilling to turn away the Arab League. Prior to the meeting, Political Agent Balfour-Paul had been assured by Shaikh Rashid that he would support the British position. However, during the meeting the ruler of Dubai remained 'hunched and hooded on his chair, for all the world like one of his falcons.'[68]

In June 1965, the twenty-second meeting of the Trucial States Council was held in the Council's new Development Offices in Dubai. Political Agent Balfour-Paul was armed with an unconditional Saudi commitment of £1 million, which together with a commitment from Shaikh Shakhbut of an additional £100,000 raised the amount available in the fund to £2.5 million pounds. Despite substantial resources now available in the Council's own Development Fund, Sharjah's Shaikh Saqr bin Sultan and Ras Al Khaimah's Shaikh Saqr bin Mohammed both insisted that the Arab League rather than the Trucial States Development Office carry out future projects. The only concession Balfour-Paul obtained from the rulers was an agreement to begin work on a surfaced road from Dubai to Sharjah. The lunch that followed the meeting was also a failure. Shaikh Shakhbut excused himself to pray and while the others awaited his return 'the mutton fat solidified and grew cold.' Looking for the silver lining, Balfour-Paul noted that the rulers had not provided any indication that they planned to denounce their treaties with Britain and appeal to the UAR for protection. Nor had they hinted that they might join the Arab League. Balfour-Paul suggested that perhaps the rulers were waiting to learn if 'they can have their cake and eat it.'[69]

Shortly after the Council meetings concluded, Sharjah's ruler Shaikh Saqr bin Sultan Al Qasimi was ousted by his nephew Shaikh Khalid bin Muhammad Al Qasimi. Nine years before, after a disagreement with his uncle, Shaikh Khalid had left Sharjah and settled in Dubai where he worked selling paint. From Dubai, the disgruntled royal nephew wrote several anonymous letters to British officials complaining about Shaikh Saqr bin Sultan's misrule. Finally, with the support of the Qasimi family and the blessing of HMG, on 24 June Shaikh Khalid ousted his uncle. Accompanied by Land Rovers carrying soldiers of the Trucial Oman Scouts (TOS), British officers escorted the deposed Shaikh to a Royal Air Force plane. Prior to his departure for Bahrain, Shaikh Saqr bin Sultan was not permitted to telephone his palace because of concern that he might exhort his personal guards to strike his replacement.[70]

Political Resident Luce suggested that when discussing the ouster of Sharjah's ruler, British officials refer to earlier attempts to assassinate him by members of his own family. Luce also advised that British officials publicize material that accused the deposed ruler of squandering revenue. In addition, the Political Resident announced that the new ruler had publicly destroyed 36 cases of whisky found in the palace. According to Cairo, the British constantly pressured Gulf rulers to stay away from 'the liberated Arab World.' And in this instance the British government had provided weapons to Sharjah's Bedouin. The deposed ruler agreed. Shaikh Saqr bin Sultan claimed that the British had conspired to have him assassinated and that he had discovered the plot only shortly before it was to take place.

After the departure of Shaikh Saqr bin Sultan, London was concerned that Iran might use the occasion quickly to seize some territory, including Abu Musa Island. Britain warned Iran not to move against Sharjah. London clearly stated that 'Her Majesty's Government would be bound to resist any such action on behalf of the new Ruler on exactly the same basis as before.'[71]

Sharjah's new ruler, Shaikh Khalid, assured Political Resident Luce that, with the exception of the Qadi of Sharjah, he would not continue to employ his predecessor's Egyptian officials. Luce reported to London that Shaikh Khalid bin Muhammad Al Qasimi appeared popular.[72] But the ouster of Shaikh Saqr bin Sultan continued to provide additional grist for anti-British sentiment in pan-Arab circles. While en route to Cairo, the deposed ruler visited Baghdad and was greeted at the airport by the Iraqi Prime Minister. Arab newspapers blamed Britain for the ruler's removal, complaining that London wished to safeguard British economic and military interests in the Gulf region and so kept the area backward.[73]

Sir William Luce told the Foreign Office that both Cairo and Baghdad were likely to continue to accuse Britain of deposing Shaikh Saqr, who was now characterized as a 'champion of liberation from British imperialism.' According to Luce, Egypt and Iraq would keep on claiming that the inhabitants of the Trucial States were angry about Shaikh Saqr's removal. Undeterred by criticism, the British continued to pursue their goal of a strong Trucial State Council that would maintain the stability of the area and prevent domination by other Arab states. After the removal of Sharjah's ruler, Sir William concluded that Abu Dhabi's ruler remained a stumbling block to a federation of the Trucial States. According to the Political Resident, Shaikh Shakhbut had an 'exaggerated sense of pride and importance.'[74]

Now Shaikh Shakhbut's relations with the newly formed Abu Dhabi Army caused concern. In 1966, British advisers wanted soldiers paid before their scheduled leave to celebrate the Eid holiday. Initially, Shaikh Shakhbut agreed, but the palace accountant did not receive the necessary instructions and refused to pay. As a result, the men left for the holiday without receiving their salaries, reducing the incentive of potential volunteers.[75]

Jordan's King Hussein, however, was more fortunate than Abu Dhabi's soldiers. In March 1966, Shaikh Shakhbut gave the Jordanian ruler £200,000 to rebuild a flood-ravaged area in the southern town of

Ma'an. King Hussein thanked the ruler for his generous gift and invited him to visit Jordan. Shaikh Shakhbut wanted to accept the King's invitation, but only if upon his arrival he was personally received by the monarch.[76] Explaining that all Jordanians had been moved by the Shaikh's kindness, King Hussein assured Shaikh Shakhbut that he would be delighted to greet him personally at the airport and that Jordanians would spare no effort to provide hospitality.[77]

Before Shaikh Shakhbut visited King Hussein, Political Resident Luce counseled Abu Dhabi's ruler to emphasize that he wanted friendly relations with the Saudis. Shaikh Shakhbut agreed, but declared that he would not attempt to purchase Saudi friendship at the expense of relinquishing any part of Abu Dhabi's territory.[78] Arriving in Amman on 24 April, Shaikh Shakhbut received appropriate honors for a head of state, including a 21-gun salute. The salute was unusual; a Shaikh in his position was entitled to only six guns. In addition, King Hussein devoted far more time to Abu Dhabi's ruler than he had earlier spent with either the Saudi king or the Amir of Kuwait. King Hussein presented Shaikh Shakhbut with a mother-of-pearl Koran and a model of the Dome of the Rock. He also vested the visiting ruler with the Nahda Order, the highest Jordanian decoration. King Hussein was favorably impressed with the ruler of Abu Dhabi and the members of his party, who had 'a simple dignity.' The King regarded his guests as typical Arab gentlemen and enjoyed their company.[79]

During Shaikh Shakhbut's visit, King Hussein raised the dispute between Saudi Arabia and Abu Dhabi over the territory of Buraimi. Assuring Shaikh Shakhbut that his position on Buraimi was completely neutral, the Jordanian ruler offered to pursue secret discussions with King Faisal of Saudi Arabia to ascertain if a solution was possible. Shaikh Shakhbut agreed and presented King Hussein with an additional gift of £1 million pounds. After Shaikh Shakhbut returned to Abu Dhabi, Political Agent Archie Lamb told him that his generosity to others was greater than his generosity to his own people. Shaikh Shakhbut agreed that it was now important for him to move quickly with development projects at home.[80]

As 1966 progressed, the British continued to express concern about Shaikh Shakhbut's willingness to carry out administrative reforms. Nevertheless, Shaikh Shakhbut's brother, Shaikh Zaid bin Sultan, was optimistic that the ruler would finally move forward. After touring the Liwa, Political Agent Lamb told the ruler that the area needed pumps and a school. Shaikh Shakhbut promised to provide them. Turning to the administration of Abu Dhabi, Shaikh Shakhbut told Lamb that

'Rome was not built in a day.' He wanted to move slowly and carefully. The Political Agent agreed that it was impossible to do everything at once and suggested that the first priority was appointment of a Director of Finance and establishment of a suitable finance department. Lamb also requested that the ruler give priority to establishment of an appropriate department of health. Since Shaikh Shakhbut was in the process of building a hospital he clearly needed an official to take charge of its administration. In addition, since the population was rapidly increasing, a department of police and a passport section were both necessary. Finally, Lamb stressed the importance of educational arrangements. Responding to the Political Agent, Shaikh Shakhbut requested a British Director of Finances and a British Director of Public Works. Lamb agreed, but suggested that the ruler hire Arabs to fill other positions. Shaikh Shakhbut acquiesced, saying that he wanted to hire educated Bahrainis 'provided by his good friend Shaikh Isa.' Meanwhile, Shaikh Shakhbut arranged to locate suitable housing for the soon to be recruited new officials.[81]

Bahrain's ruler, Shaikh Isa bin Sulman Al Khalifa, was glad to help Shaikh Shakhbut, but Bahrain did not yet have enough local personnel to fill positions in its own administration and continued to rely on British expatriates. Nevertheless, Shaikh Isa agreed to recruit some Bahrainis for Abu Dhabi. However, in previous years a few Bahrainis who had gone to work for Shaikh Shakhbut had been so unhappy with the treatment they received that they quickly returned home. One such employee stated that 'he would settle for an eternity of hell fire rather than a further twenty-four hours working for Shaikh Shakhbut.'[82]

Soon after agreeing to modernize his administration, Shaikh Shakhbut quarreled with his offshore concessionaire, Abu Dhabi Marine Areas Ltd (ADMA). Shaikh Shakhbut was upset about the location of a Dubai Petroleum Company rig, which he insisted belonged to ADMA. The irate ruler demanded that ADMA cease drilling. Political Resident Luce explained that the rig, which had so offended Shaikh Shakhbut, was not in his territory, but across his border in Dubai, a boundary which he had formally accepted in 1965. Shaikh Shakhbut asserted that he had been tricked into that boundary agreement and now repudiated his seabed boundary with Dubai.[83]

London was annoyed with Shaikh Shakhbut and HMG considered threatening to withdraw its protection from Abu Dhabi. However, doing so would provide the Saudis with an opportunity to move into the disputed area of Buraimi, which they had long claimed from both

Abu Dhabi and Oman. Hence, the British realized that their departure from Abu Dhabi would also endanger the Sultanate of Oman. London did not make the threat, but agreed that the Political Resident would visit Abu Dhabi, 'read the Riot Act to Shakhbut' and demand that the ruler respect established boundaries and not make claims beyond them. In addition, the British expected Shaikh Shakhbut to honor his previous pledge to contribute to the Trucial States Development Fund. HMG also wanted indications that Shaikh Shakhbut would work closely with the other Trucial States and support the Trucial States Rulers' Council.[84] Although he was cautioned to avoid threatening withdrawal of British protection, Whitehall instructed the Political Resident to inform Shaikh Shakhbut 'that HMG take a very serious view of his actions.'[85] According to London, Shaikh Shakhbut had freely entered the boundary agreement with Dubai. Annulling the agreement would be inconsistent with honour.[86]

Sir William Luce and the ruler's brother, Shaikh Zaid bin Sultan, discussed Shaikh Shakhbut's claim that he had been tricked into the seabed boundary agreement. Shaikh Zaid asked Luce to tell his brother the ruler that if he did not change his ways then Britain would withdraw its support and find someone else who could rule Abu Dhabi; someone who was prepared to cooperate with his neighbors. Shaikh Zaid insisted that his brother, Shakhbut, was so angry that only a direct threat to his position would move him. Shaikh Zaid stated that unless his brother quickly restored normal relations with ADMA, he and other family members would take action. Sir William had heard such statements from Zaid before, but never so bitterly stated. Since Shaikh Zaid was leaving the Gulf for a visit to London, the Political Resident asked Whitehall to discuss the problem with him.[87]

On 4 August 1966, members of Abu Dhabi's ruling family informed the British government that Shaikh Shakhbut, who had ruled for 38 years, was to be replaced by his younger brother, Shaikh Zaid. They requested that HMG remove Shaikh Shakhbut from Abu Dhabi and take measures to preserve law and order. The British despatched two squadrons of Trucial Oman Scouts to Abu Dhabi.[88] Then on 6 August, accompanied by Commander of the Trucial Oman Scouts Freddy de Butts, Deputy Political Resident Glen Balfour-Paul went to Abu Dhabi's Al-Diwan-Al-Amiri Palace to tell Shaikh Shakhbut that it was time for him to step down. 'What were in subsequent official terminology to be termed the "negotiations" between Mr Balfour-Paul and Sheikh Shakbut now started.'[89] Soon after, the deposed ruler departed for Bahrain.[90]

According to British observers, Shaikh Zaid's accession was hailed with relief throughout Abu Dhabi, but no 'open jubilation.' Apparently, many residents of the shaikhdom did not yet comprehend that Shaikh Shakhbut was truly out. The new ruler was concerned: 'Although he knows that his position is basically secure, he is afraid of the stray bullet from a hired assassin's or a madman's gun.' As a result, initially Shaikh Zaid remained within his own *majlis* under tight security and ordered that his nephews, the sons of his deposed predecessor, be barred from returning to Abu Dhabi.[91]

The British were pleased that Zaid was now ruler. Political Agent Lamb described Shaikh Zaid as cheerful and generous, a fine horseman, a leader who enjoyed his role as Arab shaikh, 'father of his people.' He was also considered 'gallant to European ladies and with a roving eye for all members of the female sex.' In addition, Lamb considered Shaikh Zaid intelligent and reasonable. Most important, he had a statesman's understanding of how to rule and a logical approach to international politics. Abu Dhabi's ruler understood the requirements of the states in his region. He told Lamb that 'HMG is the prow of my ship and the point of my sword.' However, although he wanted Britain to continue to look after his defense and foreign relations, he made it absolutely clear that he was not under British suzerainty. Shaikh Zaid appreciated Britain's role in the region, but at the same time was 'too intelligent and too acute an observer of world affairs' to expect Her Majesty's forces to remain in the Gulf indefinitely. According to Lamb, envisioning himself 'as an Arabian, rather than an Arab,' the new ruler of Abu Dhabi did not 'pander to pan-Arab sentiment.' Three months after he deposed his brother, Shaikh Zaid's subjects were already witnessing the results of development. It appeared that Zaid had successfully 'exorcised the spirit of Shakhbut.'[92]

But initially, Dubai's ruler was not pleased that Shaikh Shakhbut had been ousted. The British tried to assure Shaikh Rashid that the deposition of Shaikh Shakhbut did not indicate a change in Britain's policy of 'non-interference in the internal affairs of the shaikhdoms.' However, Shaikh Rashid claimed that the removal of Shaikh Shakhbut indicated that British protection was 'valueless.'[93] The ruler of Dubai was convinced that Shaikh Zaid had moved against his brother, Shakhbut, at the instigation of the British. According to one British official, Shaikh Rashid wished to discredit Shaikh Zaid 'in pursuit of his own ambitions in the Trucial States.'[94]

Shaikh Zaid met with Shaikh Rashid and the deputy ruler of Bahrain,

Shaikh Khalifa, on 20 August. The new ruler of Abu Dhabi assured his guests that Britain had not removed his predecessor. For several years, the Al Nuhayyan family had been impatient with Shaikh Shakhbut's refusal to change. Hence, the family had acted against him in order to save the country. Only at the last minute did the family inform the British that they had recognized Shaikh Zaid as ruler. Shaikh Zaid told his guests that he asked for the assistance of the Trucial Oman Scouts wholly to ensure that no bloodshed occurred. 'Their role was to maintain the peace and not to interfere in the internal affairs of Abu Dhabi.' Shaikh Zaid insisted that words alone had convinced his brother to leave Abu Dhabi. The new ruler of Abu Dhabi cautioned that if there were public protests about the removal of his brother, Shakhbut, it would be obvious 'to the whole world' that these protests were truly directed at him, that the other Gulf rulers did not accept him. Shaikh Zaid suggested that they carefully consider how mischievous states, including Egypt and Iraq, might use a protest to HMG. He recommended that the Gulf shaikhs abandon the concept of a public protest to London and instead discuss their concerns with the Political Agents assigned to their respective territories.[95]

While Bahrain's Prime Minister, Shaikh Khalifa bin Sulman Al Khalifa, visited Abu Dhabi, the deposed Shaikh Shakhbut remained in the ruler of Bahrain's guest-house at Rifaa. Shaikh Khalifa told Shaikh Zaid that his brother, Bahrain's ruler Shaikh Isa bin Sulman Al Khalifa, wanted Shaikh Shakhbut to remain in Bahrain close to his friends, that Shakhbut was old and ought not to be exiled far from home. Although Abu Dhabi's ruler preferred that his ousted brother leave the Gulf, he agreed that the former ruler be permitted to remain in Bahrain on condition that Shaikh Isa guaranteed Shakhbut's good behavior and that Shakhbut's two sons be refused permission to settle or even to visit Bahrain. Then, Political Agent Lamb suggested that Shaikh Shakhbut move from Shaikh Isa's guest-house into a residence of his own. Shaikh Zaid agreed and offered to provide a generous allowance of £500,000 per annum.[96] At he same time, Shaikh Zaid also contributed £500,000 to the Trucial States Development Fund. Lamb was pleased. Earlier, he had advised Abu Dhabi's new ruler quickly to signal his intention to cooperate with the Trucial Council by announcing a generous contribution.[97]

After Shaikh Zaid replaced his brother, the issue of the boundary between Abu Dhabi and Dubai remained a problem. Shaikh Rashid had proposed that the two shaikhdoms settle the dispute through arbitration. Shaikh Zaid was prepared to attempt a 'brotherly and neighborly solution.'[98] Although the two shaikhs worked out their dispute amicably, British officials remained skeptical. Balfour-Paul told London that Rashid's reconciliation with Zaid was merely tactical.[99]

Security was another issue that concerned the new ruler of Abu Dhabi. Shaikh Zaid decided to retain responsibility for defense and finance. He was determined to enhance the effectiveness of the Abu Dhabi Defense Force, ADDF. The British, though, wanted the integration of the ADDF into the Trucial Oman Scouts (TOS). Given Shaikh Zaid's interest in his own force, however, the Political Agency in Abu Dhabi advised that rather than offend the new ruler, London should suggest that the equipment and operations of the ADDF be coordinated with the TOS, enabling both forces to work together.[100] Nevertheless, Balfour-Paul remained concerned that 'the fashion for private Armies' would spread to other Trucial States, squeezing out the TOS.[101]

Three months after Shaikh Zaid replaced his brother, the British were pleased with 'his genial and forth-coming personality and his genuine determination to make good use of his colossal wealth.' However, the new Political Resident, Sir Stewart Crawford, noted that Shaikh Zaid was independent and, despite his affection for Britain, followed his own policies. He refused to put his Defense Force under the operational commander of the TOS and, from the British perspective, it seemed that rather than genuinely collaborating with the smaller Trucial States he acted as their patron, dispensing large gifts. Political Resident Crawford was also concerned that Shaikh Zaid's understandable enthusiasm to develop his territory might cause inflation. Nevertheless, Sir Stewart was confident 'that Shaikh Zaid will respond to patient and tactful guidance in the management of his singular little kingdom.'[102]

Meeting with Shaikh Zaid at the end of November 1966, the Political Agent discussed the affairs of the neighboring Sultanate of Muscat and Oman. Recently, the Sultan's brother, Sayyid Tariq bin Taimour, who was living in exile, had been interviewed by the London *Sunday Times* and had sharply criticized the Omani ruler. Declaring that Tariq was crazy to grant such an interview, Shaikh Zaid instructed the president of the Abu Dhabi municipality not to permit the Sultan's estranged brother to establish a business in Abu Dhabi. Shaikh Zaid was concerned that because Tariq had earlier visited the Trucial States, Oman's Sultan Said bin Taimour would assume that Tariq had Abu Dhabi's support. Shaikh Zaid intended quickly to inform the Sultan of Muscat and Oman that he was appalled by Tariq's behavior. At the same time, Shaikh Zaid instructed his police to keep Muscatis residing in Abu Dhabi under surveillance to ensure that they did not take part in any activity that might damage relations with Sultan Said.[103]

Shaikh Zaid stated that Sayyid Tariq was no longer welcome in his territory. Lamb cautioned that a permanent estrangement from Tariq was unwise. Suggesting that within 18 months oil revenue would begin to accrue in the sultanate and that perhaps the Sultan would use his new wealth to develop his country, the Political Agent predicted that reconciliation between the Sultan and his brother, Tariq, was possible. Shaikh Zaid now agreed that he would not permit Tariq to visit in the coming year, but would consider a visit afterwards. The ruler told Political Agent Lamb that he would appreciate continued guidance on how to deal with both the Sultan and Sayyid Tariq.[104]

Egypt's relationship with the Trucial States gained additional attention at the end of 1966 when a UAR educational mission visited Shaikh Zaid, who refused the Egyptian offer of assistance. During his meeting with the mission, Shaikh Zaid asked why Nasser had not kept his agreement with King Faisal to leave Yemen and allow free elections there. Abu Dhabi's ruler lectured his visitors about the evil of any Arab state interfering in the affairs of another Arab state. According to Abu Dhabi's ruler, if Nasser wanted respect from his Arab brothers he would have to leave Yemen. But not all the members of the UAR delegation left empty-handed. Prior to his departure, one Egyptian representative told Shaikh Zaid that he had a house in Cairo that was expensive to maintain and asked if the ruler could assist him. 'The Ruler could and gave him some bakhsheesh.'[105]

Notwithstanding fear of Nasser in the Trucial States, the Six-Day Arab–Israeli War, which began on 5 June 1967, provoked serious rioting in Dubai. Buildings housing British firms were damaged. Although the scale of violence surprised authorities, the ruler's police quickly restored order while the Trucial Oman Scouts guarded the Political Agency and other key points. Fewer demonstrators turned out in Abu Dhabi, where there was no violence. In Sharjah, the cable between the studio and transmission room of the *Sawt al Sahil* radio station was cut and in Ras al Khaimah stones were thrown.[106]

Shortly after the Six-Day War, the new Political Agent in Dubai, D.A. Roberts, wrote about his initial impressions. He was pleased that the British and the Arabs socialized freely. Officers of the TOS attended local functions and were not regarded as members of an army of occupation. There was no atmosphere of the British Club, 'the Officers' Mess, and the dominating Mem Sahib.' According to

Political Agent Roberts, 'This absence of a colonial atmosphere is priceless and must at all costs be preserved in the coming years.'[107] But contrary to the evaluation of other British officials, Political Agent Roberts was uneasy with the ruler of Ras Al Khaimah, whom he described as 'almost the caricature of an oriental villain.' According to Roberts, the ruler, Shaikh Saqr bin Muhammad, employed 'sinister Lebanese and Palestinians.' Roberts predicted that the Arab League would surely attempt to gain a foothold there.[108]

In the autumn of 1967, HMG prepared to leave chaotic Aden. Plans to do so had been announced in February 1966 by Secretary of State for Defense Denis Healey. Wishing to reassure Gulf rulers that the unrest in Aden would not expand into their shaikhdoms, in November 1967, Britain's Minister of State for Foreign Affairs Goronwy Roberts toured the Gulf States. London emphasized that the British departure from Aden in no way indicated that HMG intended soon to withdraw from the Gulf. In Dubai, Shaikh Rashid discussed developments with the British Minister and expressed satisfaction with plans for a new sewage system, airport and hospital. He also talked about his wish to improve the creek as a harbor for dhows and to build additional housing. Looking forward to 1969, when his first profits from oil were expected, Shaikh Rashid discussed the special underwater reservoir that was to be installed; the world's first such reservoir.[109]

Roberts and Dubai's ruler, of course, discussed Britain's continuing commitment to the Gulf. According to Shaikh Rashid, 'Everyone knew that the Gulf States could not defend themselves.' Dubai's ruler did not want events in Aden to be repeated in the Gulf. Shaikh Rashid declared that if at some future date Britain decided to withdraw from the region he wanted sufficient advance notice so that he could prepare. The Gulf rulers did not fear Saudi Arabia, Iran or Kuwait. They did fear the 'socialist states', Iraq, Syria, Algeria, and Egypt. Prior to his departure, Roberts tried to persuade Shaikh Rashid that there was no parallel between South Arabia and the Gulf.[110]

When Minister for Foreign Affairs Roberts stopped in Abu Dhabi, he told Shaikh Zaid that history provided evidence that 'the British were a patient and determined people who did not abandon their aims because they met difficulties on the way.' Shaikh Zaid considered British and Gulf interests identical and agreed to uphold British policy. According to the ruler, 'Under God they must put their trust in HMG for there was none other they could rely upon.' However, if he supported a British proposal that failed, 'the fault would not be his alone: it would also be HMG's.'[111]

Roberts also brought his message of British support to Sharjah. The ruler of Sharjah, Shaikh Khalid bin Muhammad Al Qasimi, observed that in Aden a republic had replaced a monarchy. Shaikh Khalid expressed the hope that there would be no such change in the Gulf. Noting that the Royal Air Force had been stationed in Sharjah for 30 years, Shaikh Khalid said that his people expected that British forces 'would stay for ever.' Emphasizing the need for cooperation among Gulf States, Roberts discussed the importance of the Trucial States Council and the Development Fund. Sharjah's ruler complained that the Council moved too slowly, that the planned hospital for his shaikhdom had not yet been built.[112]

Moving quickly from Sharjah to Ajman, Roberts met with the small shaikhdom's ruler, Shaikh Rashid bin Humaid Al Nuaimi. The white-bearded Shaikh Rashid bin Hamaid had ruled Ajman since 1928. The British representaive explained that he had come 3,000 miles to assure Ajman that HMG would continue to provide support. Commenting on the new road into town, Roberts praised the work of the Trucial States Development Fund. The British minister also praised the TOS and expressed the hope that members of Ajman's ruling family would join the Scouts.[113]

Leaving Ajman, Roberts carried his message to Fujairah. Here too he emphasized the importance of the Trucial States Council. The ruler, Shaikh Muhammad bin Hamad Al Sharqi, was unhappy with the company that had his oil concession because his shaikhdom had not yet received any benefits. He was also concerned about where to house teachers employed in his state. Roberts agreed to look into the first problem and suggested that the ruler take the second problem to the Development Office.[114]

Finally, Roberts visited Ras Al Khaimah. The ruler, Shaikh Saqr bin Muhammad, who served as chairman of the Trucial States Council, requested £3 million from HMG. Roberts said no, that British assistance was channeled through the Trucial States Development Office. In addition, Roberts advised that it was best for the ruler to confine his search for financial assistance to the Arabian Peninsula. The British minister also suggested that more capital was not the solution to Shaikh Saqr bin Muhammad's financial difficulties. The solution was to reduce his expenditures to match his income. Shaikh Saqr was not pleased; he blamed Britain for his economic problems. Roberts refused to accept such responsibility. How the ruler managed his domestic affairs and spent his income was not a British problem.[115]

Following Roberts' tour, from 6 to 8 December 1967, Her Majesty's

Political Agents met to discuss Gulf affairs. The Political Resident expressed satisfaction that Minister of State Roberts had visited the region and assured the rulers that continued allegations of parallels between the South Arabian situation and the Gulf were faulty; that Britain was determined to remain in the region. The Political Agents resolved to encourage the rulers to strengthen their administrative machinery and to widen their political base. At the same time, the assembled British officials agreed to encourage the rulers to settle their territorial disputes with each other.[116]

Thus, at the end of 1967, it seemed that development in the Trucial States would slowly but steadily continue under the traditional shaikhly families. And these families remained steadfast in their commitment to the British connection. The alliance between Britain and the seven Trucial States appeared secure.

NOTES

1. Despatch 3004, McClanahan to State Department, London, 24 March 1960, 786F.00/3-2460, National Archives, College Park, Maryland (hereafter NA).
2. Airgram G-996, Whitney to Secretary of State, London, 3 May 1960, 786F.00/5-360, NA.
3. Miriam Joyce, 'The Trucial States from a British Perspective', *Middle Eastern Studies*, April 1999, p. 46.
4. Mohammed Al-Fahim, *From Rags To Riches: A Story of Abu Dhabi* (London: Centre For Arab Studies, 1995), pp. 119–20.
5. Letter, Walmsley to Edmunds, London, 29 March 1960, FO 371/149176, Public Record Office, Kew, England (hereafter PRO).
6. Letter, Beaumont to Middleton, London, 10 February 1960, FO 371/149176, PRO.
7. Letter, Middleton to Beaumont, Bahrain, 2 March 1960, FO 371/149176, PRO.
8. Letter, Walmsley to Ford, London, 18 July 1960, FO 371/149176, PRO.
9. Despatch 295, American Consul to State Department, Dhahran, 23 May 1961, 886G.2553/5-2361, National Archives, NA.
10. Joyce, 'The Trucial States from a British Perspective', p. 46.
11. Airgram, A-6, Horner to State Department, Dhahran, 1 July 1962, 786G.00/7-1162, NA.
12. Letter, Roberts to Balfour-Paul, Dubai, 8 August 1966, FO 371/185524, PRO.
13. Despatch 22, Schwinn to State Department, Dhahran, 20 July 1960, 786G.211/7-2060, NA.
14. Despatch 200, Schwinn to State Department, Dhahran, 19 November 1961, 611.86G/1-3161, NA.
15. Despatch 201, Schwinn to State Department, Dhahran, 1 February 1961, 786G.00/2-161, NA, and Joyce, 'The Trucial States from a British Perspective', p. 47.
16. Despatch 301, McClelland, to State Department, Dhahran, 1 June 1961, 786G.00/6-161, NA.

17. Minutes of the Sixteenth Meeting of the Trucial Council, Dubai, 9 April 1961, PRO.
18. Despatch 301, McClelland to State Department, Dhahran, 1 June 1961, 786G.00/6-161, NA.
19. Despatch 10, McClelland to State Department, Dhahran, 10 July 1961, 786F.00/7-1061, NA.
20. Airgram A-1093, Bruce to Secretary of State, London, 27 March 1962, 786F.022/3-2762, NA.
21. Despatch 233, Horner to State Department, Dhahran, 16 May 1962, 786G.00/5-1662, NA.
22. Airgram A-60, Horner to Secretary of State, Dhahran, 6 June 1962, 786G.00/6-6662, NA.
23. Joyce, 'The Trucial States from a British Perspective', pp. 48–9.
24. Airgram 18, Horner to State Department, Dhahran, 10 July 1963, Pol. 2, Trucial States, NA.
25. Airgram A-52, Horner to State Department, Dhahran, 6 June 1962, 786G.00/6-662, NA.
26. Airgram A-77, May to State Department, Dhahran, 13 June 1962, 786G.00/6-1362, NA.
27. Airgram A-19, May to State Department, Dhahran, 14 July 1962, 886Q.20/7-1962, NA.
28. Despatch 137, McClelland to State Department, Dhahran, 23 November 1960, 786F.00/11-2360, NA.
29. Biographical Note, London, 30 July 1963, FO 371/168960, PRO.
30. Biographical Note, The Ruler of Ras Al Khamimah, 1963, FO 371/168960, PRO.
31. Airgram A-65, Lakas to State Department, Kuwait, 25 August 1962, 611.86G/8-2562, NA.
32. Airgram A-188, Horner to State Department, Dhahran, 23 January 1963, 786E.00/1-2363, NA.
33. Telegram 19, Horner to State Department, Dhahran, 7 November 1964, Pol., Trucial States, NA.
34. Airgram A-9, Macomber to State Department, Amman, 2 July 1963, Pol., Trucial States, NA. American Consul in Dhahran, James A. May, called Shaikh Saqr bin Sultan the most literate of all the Trucial rulers.
35. Airgram CA-1605, State Department to Jidda, Washington, Kuwait and Dhahran, 8 August 1963, Pol. 7, Trucial States, NA.
36. Letter, Hope to Greenhill, Houston, 1 August 1963, FO 371/168960, PRO.
37. Letter, Brenchley to Malcolm, London, 15 July 1963, FO 371/168960, PRO.
38. Letter, Thomas to Gwatkin, London, 19 July 1963, FO 371/168960, PRO.
39. Minute, London, July 1963, FO 371/168960, PRO.
40. Letter, Lord Chamberlain's Office to Thomas, London, 26 July 1963, FO 371/168960, PRO.
41. Minute, London, July 1963, FO 371/168960, PRO.
42. Letter, Crawford to Burton, 27 August 1963, FO 371/168960, PRO.
43. Airgram 28, Horner to State Department, Dhahran, 24 July 1963, Pol. 18, Trucial States, NA.
44. Letter, Political Agent to Luce, Abu Dhabi, 6 July 1963, FO 371/168956, PRO, quoted in Joyce, 'The Trucial States from a British Perspective', p.50.
45. Letter, May to Shakhbut, Dhahran, 5 August 1963, FO 371/168957, PRO.
46. Letter, Shakhbut to May, Abu Dhabi, 16 August 1963, FO 371/168957, PRO.
47. Letter, Brown to Slater, Bahrain, 20 August 1963, FO 371/168957, PRO.
48. Letter, Brenchley to Brown, London, 27 August 1963, FO 371/168957, PRO.

49. Letter, Slater to Brown, Abu Dhabi, 19 August 1963, FO 371/168957, PRO.
50. Minute, London, 9 August 1963, FO 371/168956, PRO.
51. Letter, Snodgrass to Slater, Beirut, 16 August 1963, FO 371/168956, PRO.
52. Airgram A-154, Holmes to State Department, Tehran, 7 September 1963, Pol. 19, Trucial States, NA.
53. Telegram 133, Horner to State Department, Dhahran, 7 November 1963, Pol. 3, Trucial States, NA. In 1964, historian D.C. Watt stated that Britain guaranteed the tranquility and the status quo in the Gulf region. Watt admitted that the British were 'in military terms, as out-numbered and unpopular as ever a European referee at a Latin American soccer international', but claimed that British withdrawal from the region would undermine the stability of the Gulf States, that even the suggestion that London was considering withdrawal would lead to unrest. D.C. Watt, 'Britain and the Future of the Persian Gulf', *World Today*, 1964, vol. 20, p. 489.
54. Agenda for Meeting of the Trucial States Council, 2 January 1964, FO 371/174699, PRO.
55. Letter, Craig to Luce, Dubai, 19 January 1964, FO 371/174699, PRO.
56. Letter, Brenchley to Luce, London, 24 February 1964, FO 371/174699, PRO.
57. Letter, Luce to Craig, Bahrain, 28 January 1964, FO 371/174699, PRO.
58. Letter, Luce to Brenchley, Bahrain, 18 March 1964, FO 371/174699, PRO.
59. Letter, Craig to Luce, Dubai, 10 February 1964, FO 371/174699, PRO.
60. Letter, Balfour-Paul to Luce, Dubai, 7 January 1965, FO 371/179902, PRO.
61. Minute, McCarthy, London, 14 February 1964, FO 371/174699, PRO.
62. Letter, Craig to Luce, Dubai, 23 June 1964, FO 371/174699, PRO.
63. Letter, Luce to Craig, Bahrain, 24 June 1964, FO 371/174699, PRO.
64. Letter, Wright to Weir, Washington, 7 January 1965, FO 371/179783, PRO.
65. Letter, Boustead to Tripp, Abu Dhabi, 22 December 1964, FO 371/179791, PRO.
66. Letter, Balfour-Paul to Luce, Dubai, 27 January 1965, FO 371/179902, PRO. (The Union of Egypt Syria was created in 1958 and dissolved in 1961.)
67. Letter, Balfour-Paul to Luce, Dubai, 3 March 1965, FO 371/179902, PRO.
68. Ibid.
69. Letter, Balfour-Paul to Luce, Dubai, 13 June 1965, FO 371/179903, PRO.
70. Telegram 570, Luce to Foreign Office, Bahrain, 30 June 1965, PRO. The Trucial Oman Scouts had intially been established in 1951 to keep order in the seven small shaikhdoms.
71. Telegram 999, Foreign Office to Tehran, London, 24 June 1965, FO 371/179903, PRO.
72. Letter, Luce to Brenchley, Bahrain, 5 July 1965, FO 371/179904, PRO.
73. Letter, Haskell to Brant, Baghdad, 2 July 1965, FO 371/179904, PRO.
74. Letter, Luce to Stewart, Bahrain, 19 July 1965, FO 371/179905, PRO.
75. Letter, Lamb to Phillips, Bahrain, 30 January 1966, FO 371/185551, PRO.
76. Telegram 35, Lamb to Foreign Office, Abu Dhabi, 30 March 1966, FO 371/30, March 1966, FO 371/185531, PRO.
77. Telegram 288, Parkes to Foreign Office, Amman, 8 April 1966, FO 371/185531, PRO.
78. Letter, Luce to Lamb, Bahrain, 25 April 1966, FO 371/185531, PRO.
79. Letter, Parkes to Stewart, Amman, 4 May 1966, FO 371/185531, PRO.
80. Letter, Lamb to Luce, Abu Dhabi, 30 April 1966, FO 371/185531, PRO.
81. Letter, Lamb to Luce, Abu Dhabi, 26 February 1966, FO 371/185526, PRO. Also Joyce, 'The Trucial States from a British Perspective', pp. 54–5.
82. Letter, Parsons to Lamb, Bahrain, 3 March 1966, FO 371/185526, PRO.
83. Minute, Brenchley, London, 2 June 1966, FO 371/185537, PRO.

84. Minute, Weir, London, 19 May 1966, FO 371/185537, PRO.
85. Minute, Brenchley, London, 2 June 1966, FO 371/185537, PRO.
86. Telegram 581, Foreign Office to Bahrain, London, 7 June 1966, FO 371/185537, PRO.
87. Telegram 371, Luce to Foreign Office, Bahrain, 8 June 1966, FO 371/185537, PRO.
88. Memorandum, Weir, 'Likely Effects of the Accession of Sheikh Zaid bin Sultan as Ruler of Abu Dhabi', London, 18 August 1966, FO 371/185528, PRO.
89. Claud Morris, *The Desert Falcon* (London: Outline Series of Books, 1976), p. 69.
90. Memorandum, Weir, 'Likely Effects of the Accession of Sheikh Zaid bin Sultan', FO 371/185528, PRO.
91. Letter, Nuttall to Balfour-Paul, Abu Dhabi, 13 August 1966, FO 371/185528, PRO.
92. Letter, Lamb to Crawford, Abu Dhabi, 5 November 1966, FO 371/185529, PRO.
93. Telegram 877, Foreign Office to Bahrain, 17 August 1966, FO 371/185528, PRO.
94. Telegram 553, Balfour-Paul to Foreign Office, Bahrain, 16 August 1966, FO 371/185528, PRO.
95. Letter, Political Agency to Balfour-Paul, Abu Dhabi, 20 August 1966, FO 371/185528, PRO.
96. Letter, Lamb to Balfour-Paul, Abu Dhabi, 20 August 1966, FO 371/185528, PRO.
97. Letter, Lamb to Balfour-Paul, Abu Dhabi, 22 August 1966, FO 371/185528, PRO.
98. Letter, Political Agency to Balfour-Paul, Abu Dhabi, 15 August 1966, FO 371/185537, PRO.
99. Telegram 574, Balfour-Paul to Foreign Office, Bahrain, 23 August 1966, FO 371/185528, PRO.
100. Telegram 125, Lamb to Foreign Office, Abu Dhabi, 19 August 1966, PRO.
101. Letter, Balfour-Paul to Lamb, Bahrain, 22 August 1966, FO 371/185551, PRO.
102. Letter, Crawford to Brown, Bahrain, 14 November 1966, FO 371/185529, PRO.
103. Letter, Lamb to Crawford, Abu Dhabi, 28 November 1966, FO 371/185531, PRO.
104. Letter, Lamb to Crawford, Abu Dhabi, 12 December 1966, FO 371/185531, PRO.
105. Letter, Political Agency to Balfour-Paul, Abu Dhabi, 18 December 1966, FO 371/185531, PRO.
106. Letter, Crawford to Brown, Arabia, 28 June 1967, Foreign and Commonwealth Office, FCO 8/44, PRO.
107. Letter, Roberts to Balfour-Paul, Dubai, 8 August 1966, FO 371/185524, PRO.
108. Ibid.
109. Record of a Conversation, Dubai, 4 November 1967, FCO 8/144, PRO.
110. Record of a Conversation, Dubai, 3 November 1967, FCO 8/144, PRO.
111. Record of a Conversation, Abu Dhabi, 2 November 1967, FCO 8/144, PRO.
112. Record of a Conversation, Sharjah, 4 November 1967, FCO 8/144, PRO.
113. Record of a Conversation, Ajman, 4 November 1967, FCO 8/144, PRO.
114. Record of a Conversation, Fujairah, 4 November 1967, FCO 8/144, PRO.
115. Record of a Conversation, Ras Al Khaimah, 5 November 1967, FCO 8/144, PRO.
116. Political Agents Conference, 6–8 December 1967, FCO 8/8, PRO.

2

Qatar

Situated on a peninsula extending approximately 120 miles into the Gulf, following the conservative doctrine of Wahhabi Islam, Qatar remained 'almost treeless' in 1961, but its capital, Doha, 'a very noisy ramshackle town,' now boasted neon lighting and traffic lights.[1] As was the case in the Trucial States at the beginning of HMG's last decade in the region, Britain continued to protect the shaikhdom of Qatar. Until 1867, HMG had regarded Qatar as a Bahraini dependency. However, a year later Britain signed a treaty with Qatari Shaikh Muhammad al Thani, a treaty which stipulated that Qatar submit all disputes to Britain, but pay tribute to and maintain an appropriate attitude toward Bahrain.[2] Then, in 1916, a new agreement between HMG and Qatar was signed; an agreement that extended British protection to the shaikhdom promising that Britain would protect the Shaikh and his subjects against aggression.[3]

In 1958, British Foreign Secretary Selwyn Lloyd had assured Qatari ruler Shaikh Ali bin Hamad Al Thani that in the event of an uprising against Al Thani rule, Britain would assist him. Britain continued to uphold that commitment and, in addition, retained jurisdiction over most non-Arab residents in Qatar. The British government wished to relinquish this jurisdiction, but not before the Qatari legal system was modernized.

In 1960, relations between management and employees at the Qatar Petroleum Company (QPC), a company that had been exporting oil for a decade, were strained. Workers at QPC sought additional compensation. When the company denied their request they called a strike. Striking QPC workers were quickly joined by some government employees. Committed to harmony in his shaikhdom, Shaikh Ali bin Hamad Al Thani agreed to pay all government employees for the days they did not work. He also agreed to pay double wages to the loyal employees of the Electricity and

Water Departments who had not joined the strike, but had remained to maintain essential services. The British Political Agent in Qatar John C. Moberly objected to the ruler's practice of paying strikers. According to Moberly, the ruler's payoffs resulted in a temporary fix to labor difficulties that needed a permanent solution. 'The regular payment of strike pay can only have the effect of encouraging stoppages later for any reason, however trivial, or no reason at all.'[4]

Labor problems increased. In March, the work of the company continued to be seriously affected by an uncooperative Qatari labor force. QPC's General Manager, George Tod, wrote to Shaikh Ali's son, Ahmed bin Ali Al Thani, requesting a meeting. Tod complained that the lack of a Labor Law further exacerbated the problem. According to Tod, 'hot heads' intent on causing trouble might soon create a situation that would force him to evacuate the families of foreign employees from the shaikhdom.[5] Meanwhile, Tod decided to reduce the company's local labor force. Shaikh Ahmed agreed that those discharged would be provided with alternative employment.[6]

Yet another strike erupted on 9 May. Among the reasons for this strike was that during a quarrel with one of the company's Indian employees, a Qatari produced a knife and threatened the Indian. QPC dismissed the Qatari. The ruler's cousin, Shaikh Khalifa bin Hamad Al Thani, sided with the dismissed worker, stating that since the Indian withdrew his complaint against the knife wielder there was no reason to fire the man.[7] Although government workers now declined to join the strikers, the strike continued to spread. Shaikh Khalifa bin Hamad persisted with efforts to convince the company to permit the Qatari who had drawn his knife to return to work. He also asked QPC to rehire several other Qataris who had earlier been laid off.[8]

Three days after it began, on 12 May, the strike became a general strike. Qatari employees of Shell Oil Company also walked out and finally, so too did government employees.[9] At this juncture, Shaikh Khalifa Al Thani requested that QPC hire the Doha Taxi Association for some of its transport needs. The Political Agent suspected that owners of the Doha Taxi Association, the powerful Al Atiyyah family, had a hand in the strike. Nevertheless, by the middle of May all parties appeared satisfied and work at the oil companies resumed.[10]

Meanwhile, the ruler of Qatar, Shaikh Ali Al Thani, was unwilling to continue carrying the burden of leadership and wished to abdicate in favor of his son, Shaikh Ahmed Al Thani. To achieve a peaceful succession, Shaikh Ali required the cooperation of all the branches of his family. The ruler appeared to be concerned that the Beni Hamad favored another candidate, his cousin, Shaikh Khalifa bin Hamad Al Thani. The Political Resident in Bahrain cautioned the Political Agency in Qatar that it was important to ensure that Shaikh Ali Al Thani 'does not manoeuvre us into a position where we appear to be taking a direct part in these matters.' Earlier, British officials had assured Shaikh Ali bin Hamad that on the day he announced his abdication and named his successor a Royal Navy frigate would be nearby to fire a salute. But HMG did not wish to have a frigate off the Qatar coast before the ruling family had finally decided on the succession.[11]

After consultation, the Al Thani family decided to offer Shaikh Ahmed bin Ali the position of ruler and Shaikh Khalifa bin Hamad the position of heir apparent to the new ruler. However, Shaikh Khalifa expressed concern about accepting the position of heir apparent before action was taken to curb the ruling family's financial extravagance. The Al Thanis were in debt to the shaikhdom's merchants, and received a growing portion of Qatar's revenue. The British Resident told Shaikh Khalifa that it would be easier to resolve the shaikhdom's financial problems after he accepted the role of heir. Now Shaikh Khalifa bin Hamad hesitated and referred to an earlier agreement that he, not Ahmed bin Ali, would succeed Shaikh Ali. Therefore, in exchange for his agreement now to take second place, Shaikh Khalifa wanted the British to provide him with 'a private undertaking' of support. John Moberly replied that 'our policy was to support a candidate chosen by traditional means and having general support within the Family, and it seemed that he would fulfill these conditions.'[12]

Whitehall wished to avoid ambiguity and the Foreign Office instructed its representative to emphasize to Shaikh Khalifa bin Hamad that when the moment arrived for him to become ruler, his recognition by Britain 'would equally depend on the agreement of the family *at that time*.' (Emphasis in original). The British wanted their assurance to dissuade Shaikh Khalifa from intriguing against Ahmed and at the same time hoped that such an assurance underlined that London had no intention of interfering in Qatari internal affairs.[13]

Meanwhile, an American Embassy official in London informed the Foreign Office that American sources had been told that even if Shaikh Khalifa bin Hamad rejected second place, Shaikh Ahmed bin Ali would be named ruler. At the same time, Shaikh Khalifa was informed that if he did not accept Ahmed bin Ali as ruler, he would be put under house arrest. Meanwhile, always aware of the importance of its more powerful Wahhabi neighbor, Qatar's ruling family sent an emissary, Adul Rahman bin Darwish, to Saudi Arabia to tell King Saud about the planned change in Qatar's government and to seek his approval.[14]

On 23 October, Acting Political Resident in Bahrain, Morgan Mann, flew to Doha for the accession of Shaikh Ahmed bin Ali Al Thani. Accompanied by John Moberly, Mann went to Rayyan Palace, where 'a solid phalanx of Shaikh Ahmad's retainers in flowing white robes complete with bandoliers, rifles and revolvers, headed by Shaikh Ahmad himself' had assembled. During coffee, the new ruler's father explained that he was abdicating because his health no longer permitted him to continue ruling effectively. He hoped that Britain would now provide his son with the same support he had received. The following day, as tribesmen swore allegiance to Shaikh Ahmed bin Ali Al Thani, an elderly Shaikh of Waqrah suddenly demanded that all girls' schools in Qatar be closed. Nevertheless, the ceremony continued. Mann reported:

> What the future will hold for Ahmad's reign is anybody's guess, but provided he and Khalifah can establish a *modus vivendi* and the latter can keep the wilder members of the Beni Hamad in order, I think the barometer is set for fair in Qatar.[15]

In December 1961, Political Resident Luce and his wife Margaret visited Qatar. The wife of the British Commandant of Police Ron Cochrane drove the visiting English lady to meet the ruler's favorite wife. En route, their car was waved off the road by policemen who were traveling on motorcycles. Shaikh Ahmed's motorcade was passing. Hence, all vehicles had to pull off the road, and their drivers stand until the royal motorcade had passed. According to Margaret Luce, the ruler traveled with so many armed men it appeared that he was going to war.[16]

Although at the accession of Shaikh Ahmed bin Ali the need for financial restraint had been clear, in May 1962, the British expressed concern that financial reform had not yet been instituted. Political Resident Luce met with the ruler, deputy ruler, and Director General of the Qatari government, Egyptian-born Dr Hassan Kamal. Sir William asked about reports that the ruler planned to increase the allowances paid to his family members. Shaikh Ahmed bin Ali replied that he did not want to increase these stipends, but as a result of continuous pressure would do so. Attempting to put Qatar's financial house in order, Dr Kamal was 'losing heart.'[17]

Meanwhile, the Political Agency in Doha obtained the results of an economic survey conducted by Arthur D. Little, Inc., which the Qatari government had commissioned. The report concluded that the shaikhdom's natural gas was an important resource, second only to oil. Further, the report recommended that users pay for their own electricity and water. Dr Kamal wished to follow through by introducing a sliding scale of tariffs which would penalize large users. Such a system would be a major step in educating members of the ruling family to pay their own bills. The report also criticized the government's overcentralization and suggested that salaries were too small to attract well-qualified foreigners. Political Agent Philip McKearney disagreed that low pay discouraged outsiders from accepting employment in Qatar. He claimed instead that 'it is the difficulty of working, leading to a feeling of frustration and hopelessness, which makes people leave and deters newcomers.'[18]

But political concerns overshadowed financial worries. In February 1963, in response to events in Baghdad (the violent end of the regime of Abdul Karim Qasim), noisy crowds demonstrated in the streets of Doha. Most of the demonstrators were Yemeni and Iraqi workers. Some carried pictures of Abdul Gamal Nasser and encouraged passers-by to kiss their photographs. One British official speculated that the ruler permitted these demonstrations in order to provide material that would please the Arab nationalist press.[19] On 18 April, more demonstrations took place; demonstrations to celebrate the tripartite agreement signed in Cairo by Egypt, Syria, and Iraq, which established an Arab Federation. Participants chanted support for Nasser and unity. They also expressed hostility towards Jordan's King Hussein, Saudi Arabia's King Saud and European colonialism.[20]

Nasser's government attempted to take advantage of popular support in Qatar, and at the end of 1963 Egypt pressed the Qatari government to provide financial aid to Yemen. A representative arrived in Doha with a letter from Egyptian official Anwar Sadat. Cairo wanted Doha to lend a few million pounds to assist poor Yemen, where a civil war was in progress; a war in which Egypt played an important role. Shaikh Ahmed bin Ali explained that his agreement to such a loan would enrage Saudi Arabia. The Egyptian representative was not satisfied and threatened the ruler that if he refused to aid Yemen then Cairo's radio station *Saut al Arab* (*The Voice of the Arabs*) would attack Qatar and its ruler. Dr Kamal attempted to convince the Egyptians that Qatar was not in a strong enough economic position to provide the funds. However, hoping to placate Nasser, Qatar transferred £100,000 to the Yemeni Bank for Reconstruction and Development.[21]

Earlier, in April 1963, King Saud had visited Qatar.[22] While the Saudi monarch was at the ruler's palace on 20 April, a demonstration occurred in front of the royal residence. Police fired on the demonstrators, killing three. As a result, protesters, organized as the Front for National Unity, called a general strike. The Arabian American Oil Company (ARAMCO) reported an increase in 'usual threats' to destroy the Ras Sanura refinery.[23] Anticipating trouble, the ruler had earlier asked for assurance of British assistance. Political Resident Sir William wanted the Foreign Office to tell the ruler that misgovernment was the cause of the present unrest in Qatar. Previously, Shaikh Ahmed bin Ali had ignored British advice to reform his government and, therefore, Britain wished to have his promise that he would now proceed with reforms.[24] According to British officials, frightened by the outbreak of violence the ruling family now appeared willing to listen.[25]

Political Resident Luce considered numerous reforms necessary, including reduction of the ruling family's share of the oil revenue, improvement in the organization of the Shaikh's administration and in the administration of justice.[26] Sir William told London that:

> The compelling arguments in favour of maintaining stability should not however obscure the longer term dangers inherent in a policy which obliges us to support a Ruler over whose internal policies we have no effective influence.[27]

Shaikh Ahmed bin Ali ordered the arrest of 18 members of the Front's leadership, including the leader of QPC's striking workers. Protest leaders had called for the appointment of Qataris to head government departments, the total Arabization of security forces, and equality before the law. In addition, the leadership demanded the trial of those involved in the shooting incident. Although Political Agent McKearney had not considered opposition demands extreme, the ruler refused to negotiate with the Front's leadership until the workers ended their strike. Loyal to the ruler, armed Bedouin in trucks patrolled Doha.[28]

By 27 April the ruler 'had the situation completely under control.' Shaikh Ahmed bin Ali told the British Political Agent that he had received offers of assistance from other countries; offers that he declined because he wished only to rely on HMG. But he warned that if in future he could not completely depend on Britain to assist him against all threats, both external and domestic, he would seek help elsewhere.[29] The Foreign Office instructed the Political Agency that, in the event the ruler again threatened to seek assistance elsewhere, he be told that only Britain was interested in maintaining the independence of Qatar and permitting the ruler to use the shaikhdom's oil revenues.[30]

At the end of April, the ruler published a proclamation condemning those who had attempted to exploit the 19 April shooting incident and requested that all strikers return to work so that together they could accomplish reform.[31] After the conclusion of the strike, Shaikh Ahmed continued to express willingness to pursue some reforms, including permitting establishment of a television station.[32] At the same time, the Political Resident advised the ruler to establish a consultative body.[33] But despite Shaikh Ahmed bin Ali's and Shaikh Khalifa bin Hamad's apparent willingness to implement reform, most members of their family remained adamantly opposed to change.[34]

Shaikh Ahmed bin Ali now wanted Britain to confirm the assurance provided in September 1958 that HMG would provide military assistance to restore law and order. Such an assurance was unique in the relationship between Britain and the Gulf States. In the neighboring shaikhdoms the British had agreed only to provide protection against external threats. During the April demonstrations, the Political Agent had speculated that the ruler might request that British troops be stationed in Qatar. Considering how to respond, the Foreign Office expressed reluctance to automatically say no. Foreign Office official A.R. Walmsley recalled that, prior to 1956, British troops had not been stationed in Bahrain, but now were there and vital to HMG's position in the Gulf. He cautioned that, 'our strategic dispositions are not immutable and we should at least give the matter thought.' But, of course, in the event of a possible threat to British and other foreigners, Sir William was authorized immediately to use British forces.[35]

London remained dissatisfied with the slow pace of reform in Qatar. Sir William claimed that for three years prior to the last outbreak of violence he had reminded the ruler that reform was essential. Despite Shaikh Ahmed bin Ali's good intentions, nothing had been done. Luce feared that if the ruler did not now act quickly he would endanger the stability of his shaikhdom. The Political Resident also expressed concern that refusal to reassure the ruler would lead Shaikh Ahmed to turn to Saudi Arabia. If this were to happen, rulers of other Gulf States might lose confidence in Britain 'and so imperil our military lines of communication from Aden to Kuwait.'[36]

Even municipal elections in Doha, held on 4 August 1963, did nothing to promote the notion that reform was progressing. The law establishing a Doha Council took into account concern that even if an Al Thani shaikh 'risked his dignity' by standing for election, he would surely lose. Therefore, in order to ensure Al Thani participation, the law mandated that the ruler appoint three Council members.[37] So little publicity was given to the balloting that, on 4 August, most Qataris were unaware that an election was taking place. Meanwhile, one of the winners announced that he had been elected about a week before the election was held. Moreover, after the election, the Municipal Council was unable to convene because the ruler had not yet appointed the three members that he was required to select.[38]

Nevertheless, efforts to reform how Qatar's revenue was allocated continued. The ruler began to pay for material and equipment he desired for his personal use, including his cars. The monthly stipend provided to babies born into the ruling family was reduced from 13,000 rupees to 2,000 rupees.[39] Then, in spring 1964, after considerable British prodding, the ruler finally agreed to establish an Advisory Council composed of members of the Al Thani family. A law establishing the Council was published, but the Political Agent in Doha was not convinced that 'the Law is worth the paper it is written on.' Recalling that, the previous summer, the ruler had authorized a Municipal Council and that elections for members were held, yet no meetings ever took place, Political Agent McKearney considered it unlikely that the Advisory Council would actually meet. Even if the Council held an initial session, the skeptical Political Agent was 'not sanguine that any good will emerge from a gathering of Al Thani, whose concern for the public good does not often show itself.'[40]

By 1964, Qatar's ruling family provided indications that members wanted a degree of independence from HMG. Qatar became a member of several international organizations: UNESCO, WHO, and OPEC. Without consulting the Political Agency, Qatar sought direct negotiations with oil companies and decided to invest oil revenue outside the sterling area. Members of the Al Thani family also decided to establish a Qatari airline and to secure traffic rights from neighboring states. London was pleased that the shaikhdom 'had shown a disposition to go her own way in various aspects of foreign affairs.' Foreign Office officials now considered the Treaty of 1916 out of date.

> Our existing position in the Persian Gulf leads to much misunder-
> standing: we are held responsible for internal mismanagement of the
> Gulf States' affairs, while in fact we have no legal (or moral) right to
> intervene in them, and we thus incur unnecessary odium: in Qatar at
> least (by contrast with Bahrain) we derive virtually no advantage from
> this situation, and we should therefore seek to end it at a suitable
> moment.[41]

Foreign Office official T.F. Brenchley stated that Britain had no
serious objection to Qatar's gradual assumption of *de facto* control over
most of her external relations. But Brenchley suggested that it would
be preferable to avoid Qatari *de jure* control. Total independence
would result in demands that Qatar join the Arab League and the
United Nations. In addition, if Qatar declared independence then
foreign states would seek to set up diplomatic missions in Doha.[42]

Meanwhile, a personal decision made by the British commander of
Qatar's security forces, Ron Cochrane, became a matter of Foreign
Office interest. Cochrane converted to Islam. In 1949, the British
officer had arrived in Qatar after the reluctant ruler was pressed by the
British to establish a reliable police force.[43] In the course of creating
the Qatar police, Cochrane gradually became close to the Arabs and
to the ruler. According to Cochrane, religion was the last barrier, and
now he considered his beliefs closer to Islam than to Christianity.
Cochrane asserted that his conversion was a personal matter.[44] The
new convert took the name Muhammad Mahdi and obtained Qatari
citizenship. Cochrane's British passport was returned to the Political
Agency. Now Mahdi assured Political Agent McKearney that he
would continue to cooperate with the British 'so far as is consonant
with loyalty to Qatar.'[45]

McKearney doubted that Mahdi's conversion was simply a personal
matter, without any sort of political significance. Another British
official speculated that Cochrane may have wished to protect his
position as head of the security forces and that, as a Muslim, he was
less vulnerable to attack by Arab nationalists. In addition, there was
speculation that, since the Gulf remained an area of great importance
to HMG, the new Muslim was in a better position to support the
British presence than he had been as a Christian. Before his conversion, Cochrane was invited to numerous ruling family gatherings and
now the retired ruler, Shaikh Ali bin Hamad, 'would to all intents and
purposes take him as his son.' Some Qataris, however, suggested that
Cochrane had been ordered to accept Islam by 'his British masters
who wish him to become more acceptable to the Arabs.'[46]

While loyalty to the ruler was not a problem for Muhammad Mahdi, in the spring of 1965 Political Agent Ranald Boyle noted that some Qataris, including many members of the merchant class, harbored 'a deep-seated resentment' against the Al Thani family. Boyle expressed concern that this resentment would lead to some sort of upheaval. And the Political Agent wanted to find a way to heal the breach.[47]

British interest in internal reform continued. Political Resident Luce expressed disappointment that members of the Al Thani family remained extravagant and showed no indication that they were exercising financial responsibility. Sir William wanted to press Shaikh Ahmed bin Ali to decrease family expenditures, but feared that too much pressure might anger the ruler and possibly jeopardize Qatari cooperation in other areas, including resistance to Arab League penetration of the Gulf region.[48]

Arab League efforts to open an office in the Gulf States became a matter of increasing British concern in 1965. During a meeting with the ruler and Shaikh Khalifa in Rayyan Palace on 13 January, the Political Resident complained that Egypt and Iraq used the League to promote goals that were not in the interest of regional stability. Nevertheless, since some Trucial States remained poor and truly needed economic assistance, London was reluctant to request that these shaikhdoms refuse League offers. Shaikh Ahmed, too, opposed establishment of a League office, which he claimed would become a center for subversion and would endanger the entire Gulf region.[49] Yet again, Political Resident Luce expressed the hope that British resistance to an Arab League office might provide a new opportunity to advocate internal reform in Qatar, including an end to 'the flagrant extravagances of the ruling family.' Luce wanted both the ruler and the deputy ruler to set an example by reducing 'their own enormous slices of the cake.'[50]

In 1965, a British visitor who arrived in Doha after an absence of ten years noted that official appointments could still be made or cancelled by a word or a signature, and that no civil service had been established, nor had a proper municipality been set up. At the same time, the British visitor was impressed by the physical changes he observed. The overgrown fishing-village of 1955 had become

> a sprawling city of concrete buildings, traffic lights, ring roads and soda stalls; air conditioning is the rule; the waterfront area has been re-claimed, and much of the filth removed; a large merchant class has grown up and social life has become conventional and 'big city'; Sheikh

> Ali, now in retirement, still wields a powerful influence over the Ruling
> Family, personifying as he does the autocratic Arab patriarch guided by
> years of tradition; . . . [51]

The ruler truly wished to achieve modernization and continued
efforts to curb his personal expenses. In September 1965, he dismissed
200 employees and closed his garage and workshops. Political Agent
Boyle decided once more to address the issue of the yet to be
convened Advisory Council. Shaikh Ahmed bin Ali had appointed
members to that Council, but as a result of conflicts within the ruling
family the Advisory Council had not convened. In addition, Boyle
wanted the ruler to call together 'the elected, but moribund,
Municipal Council.'[52]

At the beginning of 1966, heir apparent Shaikh Khalifa bin Hamad
was concerned that, under pressure from members of the ruling
family, Shaikh Ahmed bin Ali would increase family stipends from
revenue soon expected from Shell Oil. The deputy ruler wanted his
cousin to resist providing additional handouts to family members. He
suggested that, instead, the ruler put newly available resources into
the country's Reserve Fund.[53]

Some family members had recently been involved in a shooting
incident. Such behavior reduced respect for the Al Thani and
provided ammunition for their enemies. At the same time, Shaikh
Khalifa bin Ali was worried that Qataris who had been sent to study
abroad were unhappy about their prospects for employment after
returning home. In addition, the deputy ruler grumbled that although
members had been elected to a promised Advisory Council, there was
still no indication of when Shaikh Ahmed might convene the
Council.[54]

In August 1966, shortly after a visit to England, Shaikh Khalifa bin
Hamad visited Abu Dhabi; a meeting that Political Agent in Doha,
Ranald Boyle, called 'a rapturous success.' Boyle was convinced that
the Shaikh's travels had served to widen his outlook and as a result 'he
is now not nearly so much an arrogant prince, as a developing
statesman.' The Political Agent suggested that the leaders of the Gulf
be encouraged to visit London annually.[55]

Two months later, during conversations with Shaikh Ahmed bin Ali,
Political Resident Sir Stewart Crawford emphasized the importance
of cooperation among all the Gulf States. He suggested that, since
Shaikh Zaid bin Sultan Al Nuhayyan had replaced his brother
Shakhbut as Abu Dhabi's ruler, a stumbling block had been removed.

Although Qatar's ruler agreed that Shaikh Shakhbut had been an impediment to cooperation, he was unhappy that, prior to the change in Abu Dhabi, other Gulf rulers had not been secretly consulted. Now Qatar's ruler was displeased that Shaikh Shakhbut bin Sultan was 'wandering about homeless with his family and womenfolk.' Political Resident Crawford explained that events in Abu Dhabi had moved so quickly that there had not been time for consultation.[56]

The Political Resident turned to border issues, expressing the hope that the border between Abu Dhabi and Qatar would be quickly settled and so too would the sea boundaries between Qatar and Bahrain. Shaikh Ahmed bin Ali replied that, in so far as boundaries with his neighbors were concerned, he relied on the HMG. He wanted the British to hear the arguments of all the shaikhdoms concerned and afterwards to decide each case. Sir Stewart disagreed. He wanted such problems settled by the states alone and considered the idea of British intervention 'a retrograde step.' The ruler admitted that perhaps in the case of Abu Dhabi and Qatar it would be possible to reach understandings without British intervention. But Shaikh Ahmed bin Ali was not convinced that the rulers were prepared to solve their problems without British help. He cited Bahrain's insistence that the proposed Arabian Currency Board be head-quartered in Bahrain rather than move from capital to capital as Qatar had proposed. 'The Bahrainis assumed too much: they wanted the centre of everything to be in Bahrain.'[57]

During the June 1967 Six-Day War, the Palestine Liberation Organization (PLO), which had a sizeable representation in Doha, organized demonstrations. The Qatari government gave the PLO permission to hold public meetings, with the provision that order be maintained. At the same time, the ruler 'unwillingly' sent a telegram of support to Nasser and ordered payment of approximately £50,000 to the PLO. Shaikh Ahmed bin Ali explained to the Political Agency that, for both political and religious reasons, he had to support the Egyptian leader. The ruler also offered Palestinians residing in Qatar travel funds to enable them to go to Egypt and volunteer their services, 'but so far no takers.'[58] On the first day of the war, approximately 200 people, mainly Palestinian and Yemeni, gathered at the British Embassy shouting slogans, including 'beat the Consul.' Members of the crowd threw stones at the buildings and at the Union Jack. Sixteen windows were broken and the Agency's 'always too curious' Omani gardener suffered a cut on his hand.[59]

According to the Political Agent in Doha, the most potentially dangerous event took place on Friday evening, 9 June, when forces stationed at the Doha fort appeared to be near mutiny. During the course of the war they remained with little to do but listen to the radio, discuss the events with each other, and accept as fact all the rumors that they heard. Nasser's defeat was difficult. 'The downfall of their god was the last straw.' Men started to weep and 'a form of hysteria began to affect the troops.' Commanding officer Muhammad Mahdi, the former Colonel Cochrane, was hit on the neck and one Jordanian officer was kicked. Accompanied by his brother and local Bedouin soldiers loyal to the Al Thani family, Shaikh Khalifa bin Ali arrived quickly. After a period of shouting and persuading, 'the tumult died down.'[60] Political Agent Boyle reported it had been a mistake to keep a large number of 'emotional and politically-conscious Arabs' in one location. Had these men been dispersed for duty in different sections of the shaikhdom they would have remained steady.[61]

After President Nasser's broadcast announcement of his resignation, sporadic demonstrations erupted in Doha. A few stones were thrown, some windows in the British Bank of the Middle East were broken, but no major damage resulted. Despite public conviction that there had been Anglo-American collusion with Israel and that collusion was responsible for the Arab defeat, the British community remained calm.[62]

On 16 June, Political Agent Boyle reported to Political Resident Sir Stewart that during the war the PLO had insisted that all Arabs who did not support their cause were 'bad' Arabs.[63] But Palestinian influence in Qatar was limited because the ruler acted with determination. In addition, shortly before the war began, a Palestinian bakery had used flour which had accidentally been contaminated with a lethal insecticide.[64] Panic swept through Doha as 500 people were rushed to the hospital. Seven later died. Quickly, a rumor circulated that the British had poisoned the city's water. Qatar had neither a radio station nor a newspaper, so word of mouth was the primary source of information. Important announcements were made in the mosques and, in matters of urgency, were publicized using loudspeakers mounted on police cars.[65] The rumor that the British had poisoned the water was difficult to control, 'especially when Nasser had declared his big lie about Anglo-American participation on the side of Israel.' But, after experts from the World Health Organization announced that the cause of the illness was definitely contaminated flour from a specific Palestinian bakery, the rumors subsided.

The Political Agent reported that, during the June conflict, Shaikh

Ahmed bin Ali acted firmly and sensibly. The ruler expressed his friendship for Britain and his distaste for Nasser. Speaking to Boyle, Shaikh Ahmed called Nasser a criminal and claimed that the Egyptian leader 'has led the Arabs to Hell, and is taking them further.' But when addressing Arabs, the ruler played down both his pro-British sentiments and his anti-Nasser convictions. To do otherwise would have endangered his position and the security of the shaikhdom. Considering security, Boyle wanted the ruler quickly to reduce the number of Yemenis who served in his security forces and also to reduce the number of northern Arabs employed in his government. Shaikh Khalifa bin Hamad, who agreed with the Political Resident, suggested that northern Arabs might be replaced with 'quieter and more reliable people:' Indians and Pakistanis.[66]

Meanwhile, Shaikh Ahmed bin Ali advised the British on how the Great Powers ought to treat Israel:

> His views, which are not particularly antagonistic towards Israel, are that the state of Israel will continue to exist, but that the great powers must show her that she is not loved and that she cannot, despite her victory, have everything her own way. The great powers should be firm with her, and ensure that she withdraws from occupied territory and makes her first task co-operation over the settlement of refugees. As regards the future of Jerusalem, the Israelis must not be allowed to retain it. For Moslems, the city comes only after Mecca and Medina in importance, and Israel cannot be allowed to exercise full control over it. Some sort of 'international' city status must be conferred on it.[67]

By 22 June, the tempo in Doha appeared to be normal. Qataris criticized the United States and the Soviet Union, but remained friendly with the British community. Israel's conquest of the Suez Canal resulted in a large increase in freight charges for goods that now could no longer reach the Gulf via the Canal. 'The thoughts of many people are turning back to their pockets and their bank accounts.'[68] Prior to leaving for vacation at the end of June, Political Agent Boyle attempted to discuss government organization with Qatar's ruler. Boyle was distressed by the lack of interest in administrative routine, which Shaikh Ahmed bin Ali left to the deputy ruler. Shaikh Ahmed was not even aware that during the recent poison epidemic no permanent health officer was available. At the same time, he was not at all involved in securing a replacement for Director General Kamal, who was soon to retire. Boyle advised the ruler to arrange a weekly meeting with his deputy ruler, Shaikh Khalifa bin Hamad, in order to discuss matters of state and to exercise more control. 'Shaikh Ahmad looked slightly put out at the thought of this distasteful task.'[69]

Later, during a visit from Political Resident Crawford, Shaikh Khalifa bin Hamad set forth his views. He no longer wanted a single Director General of the government. After Dr Kamal retired he planned to divide the governmental structure into three separate components: finance, administration, legal. Shaikh Khalifa was prepared to pay excellent salaries in order to hire three high-powered men, and was already considering candidates from Jordan and Sudan.[70]

At the end of June 1967, Sir Stewart once again visited Shaikh Ahmed. Qatar's ruler expressed concern about the large number of foreigners residing in his country, including Palestinians, and told the Political Resident that he was considering how to reduce the number. The two also discussed the Arab–Israeli conflict. According to Shaikh Ahmed, the major problem was that Egypt would not recognize Israel and that Israel would not withdraw from Egyptian territory until receiving such recognition. Turning to the question of Jerusalem, the ruler again insisted that the Old City could not remain under Israeli control. He showed Political Resident Crawford a telegram that he had recently received from Jordanian religious leaders, which called for *jihad* to win back Jerusalem. Shaikh Ahmed expressed the hope that the United Nations would take control of the holy sites.[71]

Political Resident Crawford raised the issue of oil. After the Six-Day War, prior to exporting oil from Qatar, production companies had to sign a document stipulating that their oil was not bound for Britain, the United States or Israel. As yet, no American or British flag tankers had been loaded. Sir Stewart understood that Qatar had to appear to support Arab nationalism, and had, therefore, restricted oil exports. But the Political Resident cautioned that 'it would be unwise to take this sort of thing too far.' International companies would seek oil elsewhere and, if they did, the Gulf States, including Qatar, might find it difficult to regain their markets. 'The only sufferers in this event would be Qatar and the Qataris.' Shaikh Ahmed assured his British guest that he well understood the situation and hoped that the present restrictions on oil export would not long remain in place. The ruler also assured the Political Resident that Qatar had no wish to boycott western goods.[72]

Although Shaikh Khalifa bin Hamad had earlier expressed intentions to reorganize the government, after Dr Kamal's July departure, little was achieved. Director General Hassan Kamal had resigned his positions to live in Paris. According to the American sources, Dr Kamal had become frustrated by what he considered to be the failure of the Al Thani family to follow his advice concerning fiscal reform and future development. At the same time, he was a Francophile who enjoyed the arts and 'had wearied of residing in such a social and cultural wilderness as Qatar.'[73] According to the terms of his new contract with the Qatari government, every three months the former Director General was required to spend several weeks in Doha as a non-resident adviser, charged with the task of working on OPEC affairs, United Nations and legal matters. Hence, Political Agent Boyle was displeased that after Dr Kamal returned to Doha in October he once more worked on internal administration, including boundary problems and financial issues. Here was indication that the ruling family was once again ignoring the need to reorganize Qatar's administration. Boyle doubted that he could convince either Shaikh Ahmed or Shaikh Khalifa to change.

> Sheikh Ahmad's besetting sin is indolence, and he has, to all intents and purposes handed over all executive and administrative work to Shaikh Khalifa. Shaikh Khalifa is equally unlikely to take any clear decision, because he is basically a petty dictator and wants to have a finger in every pie. He had developed the policy of 'Divide and Rule' to a fine art, and is now regarded with a mixture of hatred and admiration by large sections of the community.[74]

Political Resident Boyle continued to be frustrated by the absence of administrative organization in the shaikhdom. Shaikh Ahmed appeared to take for granted that 'miraculously, the government structure would somehow broaden.' However, his cousin, Shaikh Khalifa, steadfastly expressed determination to make changes. He still wanted to replace expatriate Arabs who served in important positions with Qataris. Nevertheless, Boyle was convinced that the deputy ruler intended to keep all power in his own hands.[75]

Later, in November 1967, when Minister of State Goronwy Roberts toured the Gulf States, Shaikh Ahmed told him that Britain's planned withdrawal from Aden had planted doubts about Britain's intentions in the region. The ruler said he wished to be certain that Britain would remain in the Gulf and 'would not fix a time limit for her stay in the future.' Roberts assured Shaikh Ahmed that 'there was no time limit' for Britain's continued presence and that Britain was in fact increasing the number of Her Majesty's forces in the region; a clear indication of London's determination to maintain peace in the area. But Roberts cautioned Shaikh Ahmed that the rulers of the region would have to resolve their disputes with each other without 'too much interference by Britain.' Although HMG was prepared to provide advice, Britain did not wish to be perceived as a neocolonialist power.[76]

So, in Qatar as in the Trucial States, at the end of 1967, despite the trauma of the Six-Day War, the shaikhdom remained close to Britain. The Al Thani family was neither willing to relinquish British protection nor to abandon its total control of the country's resources. Therefore, traditional life continued with little interruption.

NOTES

1. Margaret Luce, *From Aden to the Gulf, Personal Diaries, 1956–1966* (London: Michael Russell, 1987), pp. 107–8.
2. Jill Crystal, *Oil and Politics in the Gulf: Rulers and Merchants in Kuwait and Qatar* (Cambridge: Cambridge University Press, 1995), p. 30.
3. Husain Al Baharna, *The Arabian Gulf States* (Singapore: Tien Wah Press, 1978), pp. 38–9.
4. Letter, Moberly to Middleton, Doha, 6 January 1960, FO 371/1149180, PRO.
5. Letter, Tod to Shaikh Ahmad, Doha, 15 March 1960, FO 371/1149180, PRO.
6. Letter, Moberly to Middleton, Doha, 16 March 1960, FO 371/1149180, PRO.
7. Telegram 42, Moberly to Foreign Office, Doha, 9 May 1960, FO 371/1149180, PRO.
8. Telegram 44, Moberly to Foreign Office, Doha, 11 May 1960, FO 371/1149180, PRO.
9. Telegram 45, Moberly to Foreign Office, Doha, 12 May 1960, FO 371/1149180, PRO.
10. Letter, Moberly to Middleton, Doha, 17 May 1960, FO 371/1149180, PRO.
11. Letter, Mann to Moberly, Bahrain, 18 October 1960, FO 371/149172, PRO.
12. Telegram 116, Moberly to Foreign Office, Doha, 18 October 1960, FO 371/149172, PRO.
13. Telegram 1217, Foreign Office to Bahrain, London, 21 October 1960, FO 371/149172, PRO.
14. Minute, Walmsley, London, 21 October 1960, FO 371/149172, PRO.
15. Letter, Man to Beaumont, Bahrain, 25 October 1960, FO 371/149172, PRO.
16. Luce, *From Aden to the Gulf*, p. 109.
17. Annex to Qatar Diary No. 4, April 1962, Doha, FO 371/162988, PRO.
18. Letter, McKearney to Brown, Doha, 16 February 1963, FO 371/168851, PRO.
19. Letter, McKearney to Brown, Doha, 10 February 1963, FO 371/168851, PRO.
20. Telegram 217, Luce to Foreign Office, Bahrain, 24 April 1963, FO 371/168851, PRO.
21. Letter, McKearney to Rich, Doha, 25 November 1963, FO 371/168856, PRO.
22. Telegram 125, Horner to Secretary of State, Dhahran, 29 October 1963, Pol. 32-1, Qatar–Saud, NA.
23. Telegram 305, Horner to Secretary of State, Dhahran, 23 April 1963, Pol. 25, Qatar, NA.
24. Telegram 207, Luce to Foreign Office, Bahrain, 21 April 1963, FO 371/168851, PRO.

25. Telegram 306, Horner to Secretary of State, 24 April 1963, Pol. 25, Qatar, NA.
26. Telegram 213, Luce to Foreign Office, Bahrain, 22 April 1963, FO 371/168851, PRO.
27. Telegram 221, Luce to Foreign Office, Bahrain, 25 April 1963, FO 371/168851, PRO.
28. Telegram 24, McKearney to Foreign Office, Doha, 27 April 1963, FO 371/168851, PRO.
29. Ibid.
30. Telegram 432, Foreign Office to Bahrain, London, 2 May 1963, FO 371/168851, PRO.
31. Telegram 25, McKearney to Foreign Office, Doha, 29 April 1963, FO 371/168851, PRO.
32. Telegram 305, Horner to Secretary of State, Dhahran, 15 May 1963, Pol. 25, Qatar, NA.
33. Letter, McKearney to Brown, Doha, 11 May 1964, FO 371/174651, PRO.
34. Minute, Brenchley, London, 21 June 1963, FO 371/168851, PRO.
35. Minute, Walmsley, London, 29 April 1963, FO 371/168851, PRO.
36. Minute, Brenchley, London, 11 July 1963, FO 371/168852, PRO.
37. Letter, McKearney to Rich, Doha, 23 July 1963, FO 371/168852, PRO.
38. Letter, Morphet to Rich, Doha, 6 August 1963, FO 371/168852, PRO.
39. Minute, Snellgrove, London, 31 March 1964, FO 371/174651, PRO.
40. Letter, McKearney to Brown, Doha, 11 May 1964, FO 371/174651, PRO.
41. Memorandum, Snellgrove, London, 14 July 1964, FO 371/174652, PRO.
42. Letter, Brenchley to Crawford, London, 22 July 1964, PRO.
43. Crystal, *Oil and Politics in the Gulf*, pp. 123–6.
44. Letter, McKearney to Rich, Doha, 20 January 1964, FO 371/174651, PRO.
45. Letter, McKearney to Rich, Doha, 31 December 1964, FO 371/174651, PRO.
46. Letter, McKearney to Rich, Doha, 20 January 1964, FO 371/174651, PRO.
47. Letter, Boyle to Luce, Doha, 22 May 1965, FO 371/179868, PRO.
48. Letter, Luce to Boyle, Bahrain, 31 May 1965, FO 371/179868, PRO.
49. Record of a Meeting, Doha, 13 January 1965, FO 371/179869, PRO.
50. Letter, Luce to Boyle, Bahrain, 31 May 1965, FO 371/179868, PRO.
51. Letter, Morris to Luce, Doha, 14 July 1965, FO 371/179868, PRO.
52. Letter, Boyle to Phillips, Doha, 19 September 1965, FO 371/179868, PRO.
53. Notes on a Meeting, Doha, 25 January 1966, FO 371/185462, PRO.
54. Ibid.
55. Letter, Boyle to Lamb, Doha, 27 August 1966, FO 371/185529, PRO.
56. Record of a Meeting, Doha, 17 October 1966, FO 371/185462, PRO. At the end of October 1966 the new ruler of Abu Dhabi, Shaikh Zaid bin Sultan Al Nuhayyan, visited Qatar. This official visit was the first by an Abu Dhabi ruler for more than 40 years. It appeared likely that Qatari–Abu Dhabi relations would be friendly and firm.
57. Record of a Meeting, Doha, 17 October 1966, FO 371/185462, PRO.
58. Telegram 4, Boyle to Foreign Office, Doha, 3 June 1967, FCO 8/724, PRO.
59. Letter, Boyle to Crawford, Doha, 16 June 1967, FCO 8/724, PRO.
60. Ibid.
61. Visit to Qatar Doha, 29 June 1967, FCO 8/724, PRO.
62. Telegram 5, Boyle to Foreign Office, Doha, 10 June 1967, FCO 8/724, PRO.
63. Letter, Boyle to Crawford, Doha, 16 June 1967, FCO 8/724, PRO.
64. Letter, Stewart to Brown, Arabia, 28 June 1967, FCO 8/44, PRO.
65. Letter, Boyle to Weir, Doha, 22 June 1967, FCO 8/724, PRO.
66. Letter, Boyle to Crawford, Doha, 16 June 1967, FCO 8/724, PRO.
67. Ibid.

68. Letter, Boyle to Weir, Doha, 22 June 1967, FCO 8/724, PRO.
69. Letter, Boyle to Melhuish, Doha, 24 June 1967, FCO 8/722, PRO.
70. Visit to Qatar, Doha, 29 June 1967, FCO 8/724, PRO.
71. Notes on a Meeting, Doha, 28 June 1967, FCO 8/724, PRO.
72. Visit to Qatar, Doha, 29 June 1967, FCO 8/724, PRO.
73. Telegram 63, Adams to State Department, Dhahran, 18 December 1967, Pol. 15-1, Qatar, NA.
74. Letter, Boyle to Balfour-Paul, Doha, 18 October 1967, FCO 8/722, PRO.
75. Letter, Boyle to Balfour-Paul, Doha, 14 December 1967, FCO 8/722, PRO.
76. Record of a Meeting, Doha, 2 November 1967, FCO 8/144, PRO.

3

Bahrain[1]

In 1960, Bahrain, an archipelago of more than thirty islands approximately 15 miles from Saudi Arabia and 18 miles from Qatar, was ruled by Shaikh Sulman bin Hamad Al Khalifa, whose ancestors had ruled the shaikhdom since 1782 when they occupied the islands and ended Persian suzerainty.[2] Shaikh Sulman and his family were Sunni, but a substantial portion of his subjects were Shia. The first Arab Gulf State to acquire oil wealth, producing commercial quantities since 1934, Bahrain developed utilities, roads, education, and healthcare before its neighbors did so.[3] However, as a result of its limited oil reserves, Bahrainis continued attempts to diversify their economy and Bahrain's ruler continued to depend on British advice.

In 1948, British official Sir John Troutbeck had written:

> In our own empire all our efforts are extended towards giving the natives more and more independence. I cannot see how we can hope to move successfully in the opposite direction in the Arab world. Whatever may be the feelings of one or two petty chiefs, the urge for independence from western rule is surely bound to grow even in these little Arab states in the Gulf. Of course the immediate result where western authority is discarded is a lowering of the standard of administration as is only too evident in Egypt. But I do not believe we can stop this by trying to put the clock back and force upon these countries British advisers with a clearly defined executive authority. They just won't stand for it.[4]

In 1956, Shaikh Sulman had requested that three men, whom he claimed were implicated in an attempt to murder him and his British adviser Sir Charles Belgrave, be imprisoned on a British possession. These men, Abdul Rahman Al Bakir, Abdul Aziz Shamlan, and Abdul Ali Aliwat, were leaders of a group know as the Committee of National Union. Shaikh Sulman feared that if they remained in his custody they would continue to be the focus of local discontent. The ruler speculated that if the three were simply banished rather than imprisoned they would go to Cairo and work against his interests. Shaikh Sulman had been London's 'staunch friend' during the 1956 Suez crisis and the Foreign Office wanted to help. Political Resident Sir Bernard Burrows explained to Shaikh Sulman that it would be easier for HMG to justify taking custody of his prisoners if first they were convicted of some serious crime. As a result, the ruler had established a special court composed of three judges, all members of the Al Khalifa family. The accused were, of course, found guilty and the three leaders sentenced to 14 years in a prison located outside Bahrain.[5] Relying on the terms of the Colonial Prisoners Removal Act 1869, an Act that was extended to Bahrain, the men were conveyed to the Island of St Helena.[6]

After arrival on St Helena, Al Bakir appealed to the Supreme Court of St Helena and to the Judicial Committee of the Privy Council for a writ of habeas corpus. Shaikh Sulman was unhappy that the appeal had been permitted, but pleased when, in June 1960, the Privy Council dismissed the supplication.[7] However, the issue did not fade away. The St Helena three continued their efforts to achieve freedom. Al Bakir wrote that he and his colleagues remained in prison because they were among the leaders 'who have awakened people of the Arabian Gulf'.[8]

On 7 April, the Judicial Committee decided that the case should be reheard; an unusual step, which indicated that at least one of the three original British judges had doubts about the validity of the detainees' imprisonment.[9] Again the appeal was rejected. After the Judicial Committee published its decision, an editorial in *The Times* of London expressed misgivings, saying that the case presented a picture of 'an alliance between the Ruler of Bahrain and the British Government to contrive special machinery for removing trouble makers quickly from the scene.'[10] Neither the British press nor the British Parliament was willing to ignore the fate of the three prisoners on St Helena. On 29 June, two Labour Members asked the House of Commons to secure the release of the detainees. Reminding Parliament that the Judicial Committee of the Privy Council had ruled on the matter, Foreign Secretary Sewlyn Lloyd demurred. However, the Foreign Secretary suggested that the case be studied yet again. The following day, the liberal *Guardian* newspaper stated that the St Helena three ought to be released. In addition, the *Guardian* expressed the hope that the British government would no longer carry out a sentence when the impartiality of a court was in doubt.[11]

Embarrassed, Foreign Secretary Lloyd wanted Shaikh Sulman to grant clemency. London considered how best to 'soften up' the ruler. Whitehall looked for friends of Shaikh Sulman who might be willing to convince the ruler to follow British wishes. Former adviser to the ruler, Sir Charles Belgrave, seemed a likely candidate, but had just published a memoir documenting his long years as adviser in Bahrain and the Political Resident considered 'his usefulness as a "softener-up" had been impaired.'[12]

Meanwhile, the St Helena three continued to raise 'their ugly heads.'[13] At the end of November, the Secretary of State requested that Political Resident Sir George Middleton inform the ruler that HMG did not wish to continue holding the men: that he could commute their sentences to exile or accept their return to his custody. Confident that even if the three went to Cairo they would do little damage to either London or Bahrain, Whitehall pressed the ruler to select the first alternative.[14]

Shaikh Sulman was not pleased. He suggested that in order to supplant Britain in Bahrain, states opposed to the British–Bahraini friendship were behind the effort to free the prisoners and had distributed large sums to achieve their goal. Sir George denied that the Members of Parliament who supported the prisoners had been bribed. Distressed, the ruler complained that London was ready to provide military assistance to the Sultan of Oman and yet would not continue to do him the much smaller favor of retaining three prisoners on St Helena. Prior to the Political Resident's departure, the ruler also complained that money was short; that Bahrain was falling behind other Arab states.[15]

After the British government announced its intention to return the St. Helena three to Shaikh Sulman, several Members of Parliament objected. They demanded that the decision be reconsidered.[16] Opposition members declared that the original trial had been unfair, that the men ought not to be returned to Bahrain. According to their advocates in Parliament, justice would be served only if the St Helena three were released and granted political asylum.[17]

Continuing British concern about the fate of the Bahraini three escalated tensions between Shaikh Sulman and the Political Residency. On 20 December in the House of Commons, Labour members suggested that if the prisoners were returned to Bahrain they might be tortured or even beheaded. Shaikh Sulman reminded officials that had he wished to torture the men, he would have done it earlier, before they left his custody.[18]

Discussion concerning the future of the Bahraini three continued.[19] Finally, on 13 June 1961, after a successful habeas corpus action, the prisoners were released.[20] Without consulting Shaikh Sulman the men were issued St Helena passports and on 14 July 1961 arrived in London. The released men were entertained at the House of Commons. 'They appeared cheerful, fit and well-tailored.' Speaking to the press, Abdul Raham Al Bakir said that in Bahrain, the British government supported feudalism. Now he and his fellows expected compensation from HMG.[21] Three months later, the Foreign Office informed the new Political Resident in Bahrain, Sir William Luce, that the government's solicitors were instructed to negotiate compensation with the solicitors representing the three released from St Helena. Sir William was instructed to explain to the ruler that paying compensation was the fastest way of disposing of the matter. Further proceedings would only serve to generate additional unfavorable publicity.[22]

Shortly before the release of the men, American Consul General in Dhahran John E. Horner paid his first official visit to Manama. Other issues appeared more pressing than the fate of the Bahrainis on St Helena. When Horner arrived, British troops, who had been quickly despatched to Kuwait to prevent an Iraqi invasion of the newly independent amirate, were in the process of withdrawing to Bahrain. According to Horner, the British Deputy Political Resident, Morgan Mann, appeared 'rather defensive.' He explained that Britain had decided to land troops in Kuwait because the British Ambassador in Baghdad was convinced that an Iraqi invasion was imminent. Horner reported to Washington:

> It is clear that the British, especially the military, were proud of their demonstration of their ability to land troops on short notice, but worried about how to extricate themselves from a situation in which they were rapidly becoming the object of Arab animus.[23]

When American diplomat Horner visited Shaikh Sulman and his son, Shaikh Isa, the ruler reiterated his friendship for the Saudi ruling family. Since the Bahrain Petroleum Company's refinery depended on imported Saudi crude oil, Horner considered such friendship prudent.[24] By 1962, Saudi Arabia supplied more than 80 percent of the crude oil that passed through Bahrain's refinery and Riyadh paid the Bahraini government approximately US$4 million yearly.[25]

Horner called Shaikh Sulman a capable ruler who had adjusted 'to the realities of Britain's ultimate power' and was not unhappy about

London's recent display of military might in Kuwait. The American diplomat was convinced that Bahrain needed Britain. According to Horner: 'Bahrain is far from being prepared to go it alone; a British withdrawal would leave behind a most fragile political situation.'[26]

Indeed, Shaikh Sulman's dissatisfaction with how Britain handled the St Helena three had no lasting impact on Bahraini–British relations. On 2 November 1961, after the sudden death of his father, the new ruler of Bahrain, Shaikh Isa bin Sulman Al Khalifa, expressed his wish 'to maintain and strengthen the ties of friendship with Britain which his father valued so greatly.'[27] Neighboring rulers offered their condolences to Shaikh Isa. Despite earlier conflict between his shaikhdom and Bahrain, ruler of Qatar, Shaikh Ahmed Al Thani, ordered two days of official mourning in his shaikhdom and sent a prestigious delegation to Bahrain to express condolences.[28] Later, writing about his father's accession, Shaikh Hamad bin Isa Al Khalifa claimed that Bahrain's youth — 70 percent of its population — 'found in their young Amir a true reflection of their own aspirations.'[29]

Shortly after the accession of Shaikh Isa Al Khalifa, First Secretary of the British Residency Peter Tripp told American officials that the new ruler was more modern than his father, but still conservative. Hence, liberal political developments were unlikely. 'He has had enough experience with the nationalist movement to ensure that he would not allow nationalists any political freedom.'[30]

At the beginning of Shaikh Isa's reign, indications of Bahraini development were abundant. The first two Bahrainis to graduate medical school, Dr Ali Mohamed Fakhro and Dr Ibrahim Yacoub, began to practice medicine.[31] The swing-bridge that connected Manama and Muharraq was replaced by a permanent structure.[32] The ruler officially opened a new airport; a facility that provided an air-conditioned restaurant, shops and a VIP lounge. He also opened a harbor, which provided Bahrain with its first deep-water jetties and was expected to enhance the shaikhdom's position as a trading center.[33] At the end of May 1962, Shaikh Isa inaugurated a new port, Mina Sulman. Iranian nationals sought employment as stevedores, but the Bahraini government was reluctant to employ them.[34] Hence, lacking a sufficient number of workers, the port was unable to commence operations immediately.

Under the new ruler, the Al Khalifa family began to assume a larger role in administrative affairs. Shaikh Isa's brother, Khalifa bin Sulman Al Khalifa, served as the Head of Finance, and in July, after two British officials left for vacation, also directed customs. American Consul

General in Dhahran James A. May reported to Washington that Shaikh Khalifa bin Sulman had little advanced education; nevertheless, through experience he had developed into a talented administrator. According to May, 'Few other shaikhdoms of the area have been blessed with Ruling Family members of similar progressiveness and promise.'[35]

Yet, there was no efficient organization of government operations. The Political Agent complained that the ruler lacked a talented secretariat. The secretariat appeared incapable of addressing the problems it confronted.

> There is no present prospect of the Ruler and his brothers being willing to take the necessary steps to reform the Secretariat and the outlook for Bahrain in the years ahead is indeed bleak if affairs continue to be mismanaged as they have been over the past year.[36]

In May 1963, the Political Residency was concerned about a growing number of American visitors, both military and civilian, who appeared to be studying the Gulf area. The Residency had excellent relations with the American Consul General in Dhahran and the Admiral commanding American Naval Forces in the Middle East. While the Residency insisted that 'we have nothing to hide from them,' these same officials did not want Americans

> to give the local population the impression that they are here to find out things behind our backs, or to encourage the intellectuals in any too revolutionary or nationalistic tendencies, as it is only too easy to do quite unwittingly if they browse about for too long in the souks and coffee houses.[37]

Meanwhile, development proceeded. At the end of 1963, Shaikh Khalifa presided at a ceremony in the village of Jasra. He turned on a switch that connected seven villages to electric power, bringing to 35 the number of villages supplied with electricity. In December 1963, a road earlier named to honor Sir Charles Belgrave was renamed in honor of Shaikh Isa.[38] Three months later, the first traffic lights in the shaikhdom began operation. Large crowds gathered to admire them.[39]

Shaikh Isa continued to be pleased with his British connection and wanted his relationship with London to continue 'forever.' At the same time, Bahrain needed more revenue. Shaikh Isa asked London to increase the payment made for British military facilities in his state; facilities that were necessary in order to support Kuwaiti independence.[40]

In May 1964, Shaikh Isa accepted an invitation to pay an official visit to Britain. Despite Persia's eighteenth-century defeat, the Shah claimed that Bahrain belonged to Iran. Hence, the Foreign Office instructed British officials in Tehran to inform Iranian authorities about the pending visit and, if necessary, to emphasize that the invitation was not directed against Iran.[41] Preparing for his visit to London, Shaikh Isa commissioned the Bahrain Petroleum Company (BAPCO) to make an appropriate film for British television; a film emphasizing the legacy of friendship between Bahrain and Britain. However, both British and Bahraini officials agreed that the film ought not to refer to the presence of British troops in the shaikhdom.[42]

Prior to Shaikh Isa's London visit, some British officials in Bahrain were concerned about how the British press would react to the Bahraini ruler. According to First Secretary Tripp, 'it seems as if the sight of a bisht and kafaya is too much for most journalists.' He asked the Foreign Office to provide 'reliable correspondents' with factual information about Bahrain. Praising a 4 June 1964 article in the *Washington Post*, Tripp claimed that it was an excellent piece and that such articles were 'too rarely seen in the British press.'[43]

Before Shaikh Isa's departure for London, British officials in Bahrain also worried about another issue: the ruler's generosity. Shaikh Isa enjoyed giving gifts. He presented watches and other small presents to every British soldier serving in his territory or merely passing through. Tripp was concerned that, while these gifts were small, they tended 'to evoke criticism among his own people.' In addition, the ruler lavished considerable amounts on family members. Some members of the Al Khalifa family spent vast sums taking retainers on trips to Lebanon or to the United States, often remaining for several months. Tripp lamented that with a party of 20 people, the ruler's wife, Shaikha Hassa, would soon leave for London's Dorchester Hotel for an indefinite period, 'which is going to cost a pretty penny.' Earlier, the ruler had been overdrawn on his private account with the Eastern Bank, an indication that he was spending about £2 million yearly. Tripp doubted Shaikh Isa had any idea about 'the value of money and of the importance of not spending up to the limit of his not inconsiderable income.' British officials worried that the stability of the country would be impaired if the ruler continued to spend large sums while his people were called on to cut back so that the state could provide welfare services.[44] Shaikh Isa told First Secretary Tripp that he enjoyed giving presents and was embarrassed if he did not. Nevertheless, he agreed to try to limit his generosity.[45]

During his visit to London, the Bahraini ruler was considered dignified and 'extremely friendly.' He was, however, sensitive about criticism of his country and, from a British perspective, continued to be excessively generous. Politically, however, Shaikh Isa appeared extremely cautious. Wishing to maintain his shaikhly regime, he was apprehensive about Nasser's influence and shied away from constitutional progress. Bahrain's ruler asked for assurance that Britain would continue to protect his state. Whitehall was happy to oblige, but wished to avoid distressing Iran. Hence, the Foreign Office requested that Shaikh Isa refrain from public announcement of Britain's reassurance.[46]

Since the demonstrations that had erupted in 1956, Bahrain had remained peaceful. Nevertheless, the police force had been strengthened and a competent special branch established under the direction of a British Commandant. The police carefully monitored clandestine movements and arrested potential troublemakers, including communists and Cairo-trained saboteurs. Meanwhile, Shaikh Isa bin Sulman Al Khalifa continued to resist steps toward representative government and prohibited expression of political opinion. Only non-political radio programs were broadcast and no newspapers were printed in Bahrain. Shaikh Isa declared newspapers to be inimical both to Bahrain and to Britain. Oddly enough, however, foreign newspapers entering Bahrain were not censored and were avidly read. Despite the ruler's political caution, evidence of modernization was abundant. In 1964, more than 37,000 children attended school, including 7,000 girls. Three professional Jordanian judges had joined the judiciary, and modern laws were in the process of being written.[47]

On 14 July 1964, Shaikh Isa met with Lord Carrington at the Foreign Office. Lord Carrington suggested that, given the limitations of the ruler's available resources, Shaikh Isa might consider introduction of an income tax. Shaikh Isa was not prepared to tax his people. He pointed out that, earlier, a modest water tax had been introduced. The result was widespread discontent. The ruler and British officials also discussed the return to Bahrain of Bahraini students who had studied abroad. According to Shaikh Isa, some of these students came home with 'destructive ideas.' Lord Carrington suggested 'that it was better to give such students opportunities for using their talents in support of the regime rather than leave them out in the cold.' Shaikh Isa disagreed, insisting that those with 'dangerous ideas' would be barred from administrative positions.[48] As a result of Shaikh Isa's concern, on the 'smallest pretext,' students returning from abroad were sometimes arrested or quickly deported. In other cases, because of alleged political activities in Cairo or Beirut, students were denied work permits.[49]

Bahrain's ruler was pleased with his London visit. Returning home on 4 August, Shaikh Isa received a warm welcome. Two days later, the ruler declared amnesty for 29 prisoners, including two men associated with the St Helena three who had remained in prison for eight years, Ibrahim Musa and Ibrahim Fakroo.[50]

At the end of 1964, Jordanian officials visited Bahrain. King Hussein was prepared to supply the shaikhdom with both teachers and policemen. Interested in replacing Egyptian teachers, Shaikh Isa was willing to accept Jordanian instructors in the shaikhdom's schools, but refused the offer of policemen. The ruler claimed that he employed an adequate number of British police officers and wanted only British police 'in positions of trust.' Meanwhile, Baghdad pressed the ruler to permit establishment of a Trade Agent in Bahrain. Shaikh Isa refused. Although he feared opening his door to Iraq, he wished to draw closer to Saudi Arabia and replied affirmatively to an invitation from King Faisal to be his guest. Shaikh Isa understood that 'he cannot put the clock back,' that it was essential to forge relationships with neighboring Arab states.[51]

Whitehall speculated that if ever Shaikh Isa were forced to choose between the British and the Saudis, he might go with the latter, who were in a position to strangle Bahrain's economy by stopping the flow of oil to the Bahrain refinery and taxing Bahraini imports.[52] At the beginning of 1965, a Foreign Office minute noted: 'It is not surprising at a time when the Gulf states are increasingly feeling the draught of Arab nationalism that Bahrain should be turning to Saudi Arabia in whose friendship she has, in any case, such a stake.'[53]

During the course of 1964, Shaikh Isa gained confidence. His first official visit to Britain had enhanced Anglo-Bahraini relations and he appeared to be increasingly popular with his own people. In the spring, winning high praise from his British advisers, Shaikh Isa commissioned an economic survey, a census and a review of education, health, and administration. The ruler also allowed a consortium of Bahraini merchants to investigate the possibility of establishing a commercial television station and agreed to authorize municipal elections in 1965; elections which would be the first in eight years. In addition, he agreed to the introduction of the first Bahraini currency, scheduled to replace the Indian Gulf rupee in 1965. The new currency was to be backed by Bahraini reserves in Britain. Shaikh Isa also consented to a complete Bahraini takeover of responsibility for all postal services.[54]

Yet 1964 provided evidence of continuing danger from Arab nationalism. The Voice of the Arabs persisted in attacks on the government of Bahrain, and journalists from the UAR and Kuwait wrote 'mendacious accounts' about the shaikhdom. In addition, Bahraini authorities found evidence of subversive activities sponsored by nationalists from the UAR, Kuwait, and Iraq, who had entered the country illegally. Given the efforts of these nationalists, 'it is remarkable that there were no disturbances or major acts of sabotage during the year.' Attempting to calm nationalist opinion, Shaikh Isa agreed to host a meeting of the Arab Boycott of Israel conference. However, despite strong pressure, he refused to permit the establishment of a permanent South Gulf Boycott Office in his territory. Meanwhile, Bahrain continued to quarrel with Qatar, but relations with Saudi Arabia remained cordial.[55]

Calm was shattered in 1965. Dissatisfaction was expressed by some segments of society, especially the young; those under age 30 who composed 75 percent of the population. During March and April, strikes occurred at BAPCO and demonstrations followed.[56] Neither the British nor the government of Bahrain had anticipated these events. Initially, it appeared that the demonstrations were directed against a BAPCO redundancy program, but quickly demonstrators, including schoolboys, workers and government employees, succeeded in disrupting many aspects of daily life. Port operations were curtailed, bus service disrupted, shops closed.[57] On one occasion, schoolboys in Muharraq refused to return to classes after a mid-morning break. Carrying a UAR flag and banners protesting BAPCO's redundancy program, they called on workers to strike. After police arrived they dispersed, but later students at Manama secondary school attempted a similar demonstration. The boys threw stones at the police and did not disperse until the police used smoke canisters.[58] On 13 March, approximately 500 boys, joined by a few girls, threw stones and set several European-owned cars on fire. At the same time, agitators intimidated BAPCO workers. The ruler announced on the radio that he was establishing a special committee to investigate complaints against BAPCO. He also asked workers to return to their jobs.[59]

According to British officials, the demonstrations were sparked by the Bahrain Arab Nationalist Movement, which received support from Iraq and the UAR.[60] Discussing events in Bahrain, on 28 March the *Observer* (London) warned that it was unwise to suppress a reform movement.[61] Shaikh Isa was 'very anxious' that the police alone should handle the situation, but what was the ruler to do if his police force was unable to restore order?[62]

Political Resident Luce requested that the Foreign Office immediately authorize him to commit British troops to quell the riots if it appeared that Bahrain's police could not accomplish the task. In December 1964, HMG had renewed that confidential undertaking, providing that on the basis of existing treaties Britain would help maintain Bahrain's independence. This undertaking extended to assistance against either external or internal attack. The Foreign Office granted Sir William permission to use British troops if he deemed it necessary. In the event that demonstrations could not be put down by the ruler, Britain had 'a clear obligation' to provide help. In addition, the Foreign Office considered it essential to safeguard British lives. Bahrain did not have an army. If the British-officered Bahraini police lost control of the situation there was no alternative but to use British troops.[63]

Prior to the protest, British officials had been aware of the existence of an organization located in Kuwait which intended to subvert the Gulf shaikhdoms. This group, which included Bahraini exiles residing in Kuwait, was closely associated with Egyptian intelligence. The British had expected these Arab nationalists to orchestrate disturbances, but not until May when it had been predicted they would first stir up trouble in the Trucial States. However, the Kuwaiti group had established a 'fairly effective' organization in Bahrain on a cell basis and were joined by the remnant of a Ba'athist group as well as a Moscow-trained communist.[64]

As rioting spread, Bahrain's police used tear-gas grenades. The American Consul General in Dhahran reported to Washington that British naval helicopters dropped 'vomit' gas on demonstrators in Muharraq.[65] While the methods used to put down the demonstrations may have appeared harsh to outsiders, Sir William defended both the ruler and HMG. According to Luce:

> The Ruler's gentle and kindly nature has made him hesitate, perhaps to his credit, to use the tough methods which many Arab rulers would employ to deal with such disturbances. At the same time he has neither the experience nor the organization behind him to devise and execute promptly subtler and more positive measures to counter the threat.[66]

The Political Resident took pains to explain that action taken against demonstrators was measured and prudent. Sir William insisted that 'there is no truth whatever in the rumour that shots have been fired from the helicopters.' The Political Resident told the Foreign

Office that a British naval helicopter was used by the Bahrain police to spot concentrations of demonstrators, that smoke canisters were used because police in helicopters considered those canisters the 'most humane and effective way of dispersing the crowds.' Luce explained that prior to the use of smoke canisters, riot guns had been employed. As a result, on 14 March, 3 people were killed and 15 injured. The following day, after smoke canisters were utilized, there were no deaths and only 6 injuries.[67]

Riots pointed to the inadequacy of Bahrain's public relations. Now the ruler admitted that he needed a trained expert to assist him. Shaken, Shaikh Khalifa bin Sulman Al Khalifa too was prepared to think about change, even publication of a daily local newspaper.[68] But during the demonstrations the government made no attempt to weed out troublemakers or to investigate the role of teachers. Instead, schools were closed.[69]

Meanwhile, Bahraini students studying in Egypt sent a telegram to the Kuwaiti National Assembly asking Kuwait to support the people of Bahrain against oppressive British forces. The Kuwaiti Assembly replied with a condemnation of the 'ferocious acts' carried out by 'imperialist British forces in Bahrain.' The Assembly also asked the government to help the Arab League support their 'Bahraini brothers.'[70] Shaikh Isa expressed anger with the Kuwaiti Parliament for endorsing such a resolution and anger at Kuwait's government-controlled radio, which had publicized it.[71]

Events in Bahrain frightened some neighboring rulers. British officials assured these shaikhs that HMG was committed to defending the Gulf. However, London was convinced that shaikhly willingness to permit change was essential. Hence the Foreign Office emphasized that British officials would continue to urge Gulf rulers to modernize their administrations.[72] By the evening of 14 March, it appeared that the Bahraini police were in control. However, gangs of young men continued to throw stones at windows and cars. Expatriate employees stayed on site at BAPCO but, intimidated by threats to themselves and their families, Bahraini workers remained at home.[73]

At this juncture, the Queen Elizabeth's consort Prince Philip visited Bahrain. To ensure the Prince's safety:

> A rather splendid Irish group captain had guarded the airfield quite perfectly: everyone with rifles at the ready, even a machine-gun pointing out to sea, as for a sea-borne invasion. On arrival Prince Philip said 'I hope I'm not interrupting a war.[74]

Shaikh Isa hosted a dinner for the visiting Prince, where he presented his royal guest with a gold sword, a pair of falcons and two bustards.[75]

Meanwhile, Britain, of course, wished to continue to contain Nasser's influence in the Gulf, and in spring 1965 asked Shaikh Khalifa to what extent Bahrain would cooperate to exclude an Arab League presence. The ruler's brother replied that Bahrain would act together with other Arab Gulf States but did not wish to be isolated from these states, to be singled out as the foremost Arab Gulf State to support Britain against UAR penetration.[76]

By the end of March 1965, most of the leaders of the demonstrations had been arrested. Shops opened and residents proceeded with their daily routines.[77] The ruler permitted the release of some prisoners on bail. Bahrain radio requested that students return to school, workers to work and merchants to their businesses. Nevertheless, few teachers appeared in their classrooms, few workers arrived at their jobs, and most shops remained closed.[78] But Bahrain remained quiet and in May the Foreign Office withdrew permission to use British troops.[79]

Bahraini authorities wished students to sit for final examinations, and schools attempted to prepare students for these examinations. Girls attended in large numbers; boys did not. As a result, policemen were stationed at schools and attendance improved. The British suggested that in order to avoid a recurrence of school demonstrations prior to the beginning of the fall term, the Bahraini government should screen both teachers and students.[80]

During the summer of 1965, local elections were held in Bahrain's capital Manama. Alas, the elections were 'farcical.' Five thousand residents, all those paying municipal taxes, were eligible to vote. But so little information about the impending election had been distributed that only 380 votes were cast. As a result, local elections that had been scheduled to take place in Muharraq and in some villages were postponed. Director of Information Shaikh Mohammed bin Mubarak now called for the establishment of a committee to publicize elections and set up a program explaining voting procedures to potential voters.[81]

Meanwhile, the threat of anti-government demonstrations remained. At the beginning of the school term, in October 1965, the Education Department warned students to avoid mischief, to concentrate on their studies. Some students, however, did not heed the warning and stoned British vehicles.[82] In the months that followed, Bahraini authorities remained alert to the possibility of renewed violence.

In November, soon after assuming his new post as Political Agent in Bahrain, Anthony Parsons recorded his first impression of the shaikhdom. Parsons was impressed by the intelligence and charm of members of the Al Khalifa family, which occupied a 'sprawling' complex containing 600 people, 'who depend largely on the Ruler's payroll and who occupy most of the top governmental posts.' Parsons was less impressed with the merchant community, suggesting that, while the merchants prospered from the entrepôt trade, they contributed little to the country and did not wish to change. Now, with the decline of the entrepôt trade, they were looking for scapegoats.[83] Meanwhile, most business activities were unregulated by the government, and the state provided considerable support for private enterprise. A port ordinance issued in 1964 reaffirmed an earlier decree that had eliminated all tariffs and duties on goods entering Bahrain for re-export.[84]

Political Agent Parsons was concerned about the large mass of disaffected young men, 'allergic to manual or artisan work,' who considered good jobs a right. At the same time, he noted that the British themselves continued to provide an 'obvious target' for Bahraini dissatisfaction. British expatriates still held a substantial number of high governmental posts.

> With notable exceptions, their quality is low, they are too old and are obviously hanging on like grim death to their power, prestige and salaries. It is no secret that, in three or four important Departments, principally the Government Secretariat, the Bahraini No. 2s have been doing the job for years and the British Heads of Departments are only aging and incompetent dinosaurs.[85]

In February 1966, Parson's attention turned to personal matters. In the Bahrain State Hospital his wife gave birth to the couple's fourth child, a daughter named Laila. The female members of the Al Khalifa family visited mother and child.[86] When Laila was born, Shaikh Isa was hunting in Saudi Arabia, now his shaikhdom's best customer, which accepted approximately 52 percent of the value of goods exported from the port of Mina Sulman.[87] From Saudi Arabia, Shaikh Isa sent a telegram to Political Agent Parsons saying: 'Congratulations: bad luck.'[88]

Shaikh Isa might also have considered bad luck the February 1966 announcement of Secretary of State for Defense Denis Healey that a major revision of British defense policy was in the works; Britain would severely reduce its military commitment, end its treaties of protection with the states of the South Arabian Federation, and withdraw from Aden colony by the end of 1968. Reaction in Bahrain was sharp. Shaikh Khalifa told the Political Agent that Bahrainis were not certain if they ought to continue to trust Britain.[89] And the Bahraini ruler asked the Political Resident if this announcement indicated that Britain also intended to leave the Gulf. Sir William told the unhappy ruler that 'I could assure him absolutely that HMG were determined to continue to meet their obligations in the Gulf.' As a result of withdrawal from Aden, Britain wished to move additional forces to Bahrain and was pleased that Shaikh Isa agreed. At the same time, Sir William stated:

> None of us could tell what would happen after ten, twenty or thirty years, but for as long as it was possible to see into the future of such matters he could be assured that there would be no change of policy.[90]

Shaikh Isa was comfortable with the placement of a substantial number of British forces in his state. *The Economist* (London), however, had reservations about moving troops from Aden to Bahrain. According to an article published on 5 March 1966, the British troops might be entering a 'hornets' nest.'[91]

The British remained apprehensive about the possibility of violence. Since the Shia holiday on the tenth of Muharram had in the past led to unrest, in May 1966 the Political Agency noted that the annual processions took place without incident. Anthony Parsons reported to London that

> The processions themselves were orderly and the discipline of the participants remarkable. In their tight black tee-shirts and trousers the muscular young Shia chest beaters and flagellaters, executing the symbolic movements of the ceremonies with paradeground precision, were more reminiscent of the Hitler Youth than of anything I have seen in the Arab world.[92]

In May 1966, Shaikh Khalifa traveled to London with Bahraini Director of Finance Sayyid Mahmoud Alawi for talks with the British government. Discussions dealt with numerous aspects of Anglo-Bahraini relations. During these discussions the British agreed to make a substantial annual grant-in-aid to the shaikhdom.[93]

Development proceeded. In 1966, the Kanoo family partnership was chartered by the ruler as the first limited liability company in Bahrain. One of the most prominent merchant families in the state, the Kanoos, together with the Al Moayyeds, the Yateems, the Zayanis and the Fakhroos controlled major business activity in both Manama and Muhurraq. Members of these families were Sunni Muslims, heirs of the pearl merchants and dhow owners of an earlier era. Since marrying first cousins was the norm, their wealth had remained within the family.[94]

In July 1966, Political Agent Parsons remarked on the traditional midsummer quiet. Schools were closed and prosperous Bahrainis had departed for Lebanon and Europe. The atmosphere was relaxed, but Parsons worried about the future. He anticipated that the following year thousands of Bahraini young men would complete their studies, but be unable to find employment.[95]

Then, in the autumn, the British-run Flight Information Center in the Bahrain control tower became a new issue of concern. During a visit to the Foreign Office on 8 November, Shaikh Khalifa bin Sulman Al Khalifa complained that each week an Israeli plane communicated with the Bahrain control tower. Since control towers in other Arab states picked up signals from Bahrain, Shaikh Isa's government had received numerous letters from the Israel Boycott Office attacking the Al Khalifa family for communicating with the enemy. Under international agreements the Flight Information Center had no right to exclude any aircraft, regardless of nationality. Sovereign rights over the use of airspace were vested in the individual states, but the Israeli flights concerned did not pass through Arab airspace. Nevertheless, these flights did briefly traverse the Bahrain Flight Information Region and, therefore, communication was mandatory. The Foreign Office wanted the Bahraini delegation to the next Arab Boycott Committee meeting to inform the organization that these Israeli flights crossed two major air routes eastwards to Pakistan and India. If the Israeli planes did not maintain radio contact with Bahrain the life of every passenger on these routes would be in jeopardy. Hence, nothing could be done to exclude these flights from contact with the Bahrain control tower.[96]

As a result of his strong ties to Britain, Shaikh Isa had earlier been a target of Arab propaganda. Now, the ruler's inability to cooperate with the Boycott Office gave Arab nationalists additional ammunition to use against him. The issue could also be used against Britain. According to the Foreign Office, 'nothing could be more damaging to our already delicate position in the Gulf than for it to become mixed up in the Arab–Israeli conflict.'[97]

Meanwhile, the British continued to press for reform inside the shaikhdom. After Political Agent Parsons had returned from leave in

October 1966, the ruler told him that he had decided to sign an administrative reform decree, but was unwilling to announce exactly when he would do so. The Political Agent's 'optimism took a nose dive' after the ruler failed to sign the decree as a parting gift for retiring Political Resident Luce.[98]

It seemed to Political Agent Parsons that Shaikh Isa had been prepared to sign the reform decree before an article criticizing his administration appeared in the *Sunday Mirror* (London). According to Parsons, the ruler was so furious about the article that he did not wish to take a step which might look like submission to the paper's criticism. Nevertheless, Parsons was pleased that after the death of the recently appointed Director of Customs, Mohammed Saie, a young man of considerable promise and the first Bahraini to hold that position, the ruler agreed to create a new directorate general to supervise two ports and the Customs Department. Shaikh Isa appointed Shaikh Khalid bin Mohammed Al Khalifa to the post of Director General, 'who is one of the best and most progressive of the Al-Khalifah.' Parsons also noted that the newly appointed head of the Immigration Department was Shaikh Mohammed bin Khalifa, 'perhaps, the most high-powered of the young shaikhs.' The new head of immigration had taken a course at Hendon Police College and had also studied at Sandhurst.[99]

Reforms were slowly being introduced when once again, in Bahrain as in the rest of the Arab world, the Arab–Israeli conflict assumed center stage. Immediately after the Six-Day War erupted, in June 1967, the ruler's son, Shaikh Hamad bin Isa Al Khalifa, a student at a British military college, 'had high hopes that I would see my brothers celebrate victory in the streets and squares of our Holy Jerusalem.' Instead, while watching British television Shaikh Hamad witnessed an Israeli victory parade. 'A sense of bitterness and sorrow shook me to the roots during my days at the college and thereafter.'[100]

Although demonstrations took place in Manama and in the country's second largest city, Muharraq, the ruler skillfully controlled his people. As tension mounted, Shaikh Isa prevented participants in an angry crowd from sacking the British Political Agency by 'singlehandedly compelling them to disperse.'[101] When radio stations throughout the Arab world spread what became known as the Big Lie, reports that the United States and Britain participated in the 6 June Israeli airforce attack on Egyptian bases, angry crowds surrounded the Political Agency. Just as it seemed that the crowd was poised to storm the Agency, Shaikh Isa arrived in a large black automobile. The ruler stood on the hood of his car and ordered the crowd to disband. According to Parsons:

> He reentered the car which drove off in the direction of the town at a walking pace. The large crowd followed quietly: ten minutes later the open space in front of the Agency was empty: we relaxed and returned to our normal work.[102]

In addition, the presence of a British battalion on the island remained a deterrent.[103] Sir Stewart Crawford, who had replaced retiring Political Resident Sir William Luce, reported to London, in August 1967, that Bahrain was calm, that there was no problem bunkering either American or British naval vessels, nor any difficulty delivering oil. Neither was there evidence of a commercial boycott of British goods. Of course, it was extremely hot and schools were closed. However, British representatives throughout the Gulf reported that the Arabs were shocked at 'the strength of pro-Israel sentiments in Britain.' The Political Resident warned that as the Gulf States developed, public opinion would support oil restriction as a weapon to assist the Arab cause.[104]

Britain did not want events outside of the shaikhdom to distract attention from the process of modernization. In January 1967, Shaikh Isa and his Director of Customs and Ports had met with Saudi representatives to consider building a causeway to link the two states.[105] British officials praised the ruler of Bahrain, whom they considered the Gulf ruler least resistant to changes urged by HMG.[106]

Then, in 1967, alcohol consumption became an issue. According to Bahrain's regulation of 1954, anyone wishing to sell alcohol to Europeans was permitted to do so after obtaining a permit from the Political Agent. With each passing year the number of offshore drilling company employees increased, and many of these men spent their free days in Manama, where they drank far too much and sometimes became involved in drunken brawls. To prevent disorder, the Political Agent wanted to exercise additional control. The matter appeared urgent and the Political Agency imposed new rules. Alcohol was to be sold only to those over the age of 18 and was to be denied to anyone obviously drunk.[107]

When Minister of State for Foreign Affairs Goronwy Roberts visited Bahrain at the end of October 1967 to assure Shaikh Isa that Britain would maintain its presence in the Gulf, he emphasized that HMG had a large investment in the region. Roberts pointed out that HMG was increasing forces in both Bahrain and Sharjah. The ruler explained to Roberts that he was concerned about some reports in the British press, particularly about parallels drawn between South Arabia and the Gulf. The minister told Shaikh Isa 'there was no need to pay too much attention to the British press.' Roberts was confident that if modernization continued there was no danger of a second South Arabia occurring in the Gulf.[108]

At this juncture, the ruler's brother, Shaikh Khalifa, became increasingly concerned about the Iranian claims to Bahrain. He wanted London to take action to end such claims and told Minister Roberts, 'It would not help the area to become stable if Iran swallowed up Bahrain as soon as Her Majesty's Government withdrew.' Roberts repeated his message, insisting that Britain would remain in the Gulf.[109]

Bahrain, like Qatar and the Trucial States, continued to rely on HMG. At the end of 1967, the Al Khalifa family remained afraid of the possibility of further unrest inside the shaikhdom. At the same time, Bahrain's rulers had continually to take Iranian intentions into account. The British protective umbrella still appeared essential to the welfare of the shaikhdom and the security of the traditional establishment.

NOTES

1.   Material contained in pp. 84–8 has previously appeared in Miriam Joyce, 'The Bahraini Three on St Helena 1956–61: An Incident in British Gulf Relations', *The Middle East Journal*, Autumn 2000.
2.   Visit of the Ruler of Bahrain, Brief No. 1, London, 1964, FO 371/174547, Public Record Office, Kew (hereafter PRO).
3.   Donald Hawley, *The Trucial States* (London: George Allen & Unwin, 1970), pp. 258–9.
4.   Letter, Troutbeck to Burrows, Cairo, 8 April 1948, FO 371/68319, PRO.
5.   Memo, Bahraini Prisoners on St Helena, London, 30 September 1960, FO 371/149133, PRO.
6.   Case for the Respondents, Record 43, St Helena, 1959, FO 371/149129, PRO.
7.   Memo, Bahraini Prisoners on St Helena, London, 30 September 1960, FO 371/149133, PRO.
8.   Letter, Al Bakir to Chasworth, St Helena, 30 June 1960, FO 371/149132, PRO.
9.   Letter, Rushford to Beaumount, London, 22 April 1960, PRO.
10. Despatch 3501, McClanahan to State Department, London, 8 June 1960, 746D.00/6-860, National Archives, College Park, MD (hereafter NA).
11. Despatch107, McClanahan to State Department, London, 14 July 1960, 746D.00/7-1460, NA.
12. Memo, Bahraini Prisoners on St Helena, London, 30 September 1960, FO 371/149133, PRO.
13. Letter, Marshall to Ford, London, 7 November 1960, FO 371/149133, PRO.

14. Letter, Foreign Office to Middleton, London, 29 November 1960, FO 371/149133, PRO.
15. Record of a Conversation, Bahrain, 15 December 1960, FO 371/149134, PRO.
16. Telegram, Colonial Secretary to St Helena, London, 21 December 1960, FO 371/149134, PRO.
17. Draft Telegram, Foreign Office to Bahrain, 21 December 1960, FO 371/149134, PRO.
18. Despatch 172, McClelland to State Department, Dhahran, 10 January 1961, 746D.00/1-1061, NA.
19. Despatch 1756, American Embassy to State Department, London, 15 March 1961, 746D.00/3-1561, NA.
20. Despatch 2426, McClanahan to State Department, London, 26 June 1961, 746D.00/6-2661, NA.
21. Airgram 132, McClanahan to State Department, London, 20 July 1961, 746D.00/7-2061, NA.
22. Letter, Foreign Office to Luce, London, 17 October 1961, FO 371/156750, PRO.
23. Despatch 16, Horner to State Department, Dhahran, 17 July 1961, 746D.100/7-1761, NA.
24. Ibid.
25. Fred H. Lawson, *Bahrain: The Modernization of Autocracy* (Boulder, CO: Westview, 1989), p. 94.
26. Despatch 16, Horner to State Department, Dhahran, 17 July 1961, 746D.100/7-1761, NA.
27. Telegram 762, Luce to Foreign Office, Bahrain, 2 November 1961, PRO.
28. Letter, Luce to Home, Bahrain, 18 November 1961, FO 371/156757, PRO.
29. Hamad bin Isa Al Khalifa, *First Light: Modern Bahrain and its Heritage* (London: Kegan, 1994), p. 63.
30. Despatch 128, McClelland to State Department, Dhahran, 2 December 1961, 746D.11/12-261, NA.
31. Khalil Al Muraikhi, *Glimpses of Bahrain from its Past*, (Bahrain, Ministry of Information), p. 189.
32. Michael Jenner, *Bahrain: Gulf Heritage in Transition* (London: Longman, 1984), p. 43.
33. Despatch 136, McClelland to State Department, Dhahran, 6 December 1961, 746D.11/12-661, NA.
34. Airgram A-66, May to Secretary of State, Dhahran, 9 June 1962, 746D.11/6-962, NA.
35. Airgram A-47, May to Secretary of State, Dhahran, 25 July 1962, 746D.13/7-2562, NA.
36. Bahrain: Annual Review For 1963, Tripp to Butler, Bahrain, 1 January 1964, FO 371/174519, PRO.
37. Letter, Brown to Balfour-Paul, Bahrain, 18 May 1963, FO 371/168627, PRO.
38. Bahrain Monthly Diary, 1–31 December 1963, FO 371/174520, PRO.
39. Bahrain Monthly Diary, 1–31 March 1964, FO 371/174520, PRO.
40. Letter, Luce to Brenchley, Bahrain, 17 June 1964, FO371/174547, PRO.
41. Telegram 458, Foreign Office to Tehran, London, 7 May 1964, FO 371/174546, PRO.
42. Letter, Tripp to Snellgrove, Bahrain, 25 May 1964, FO 371/174546, PRO.
43. Letter, Tripp to Snellgrove, Bahrain, 23 June 1964, FO 371/174547, PRO.
44. Letter, Tripp to Luce, Bahrain, 20 June 1964, FO 371/174548, PRO.
45. Letter, Tripp to Luce, Bahrain, 30 June 1964, FO 371/174548, PRO.
46. Brief 2, Visit Of The Ruler Of Bahrain, London, 1964, FO 371/174547, PRO.
47. Brief 1, Visit Of The Ruler Of Bahrain, London, 1964, FO 371/174548, PRO.

48. Record of a Conversation, London, 15 July, 1964, FO 371/174548, PRO.
49. Mohamed Rumaihi, *Bahrain: Social and Political Change Since the First World War* (Kuwait: University of Kuwait Press, 1975), p. 301.
50. Bahrain Monthly Diary, 1–31 August 1964, FO 371/174520, PRO.
51. Letter, Tripp to Luce, Bahrain, 2 December 1964, FO 371/174522, PRO.
52. Minute, Morphet, London, 7 December 1964, FO 371/174522, PRO.
53. Minute, Morphet, London, 19 January 1965, FO 371/179791, PRO.
54. Annual Review of Bahrain Affairs, 1964, Bahrain, FO 371/179787, PRO.
55. Ibid.
56. Letter, Parsons to Luce, Bahrain, 2 January 1966, FO 371/185327, PRO.
57. Telegram 35, Tripp to Foreign Office, Bahrain, 19 March 1965, FO 371/179788, PRO.
58. Telegram 26, Tripp to Foreign Office, Bahrain, 12 March 1965, FO 371/179788, PRO.
59. Telegram 28, Tripp to Foreign Office, Bahrain, 14 March 1965, FO 371/179788, PRO.
60. Memorandum, Minister of State's Visit to the Persian Gulf, 9–16 May 1965, FO 371/179790, PRO.
61. Rumaihi, *Bahrain: Social and Political Change since the First World War*, p. 303.
62. Telegram 186, Luce to Foreign Office, Bahrain, 13 March 1965, FO 371/179788, PRO.
63. Memorandum, Disturbances in Bahrain, March 1965, FO 371/179788. PRO.
64. Telegram 205, Luce to Foreign Office, Bahrain, 19 March 1965, FO 371/179788, PRO.
65. Telegram 745, Stewart to Foreign Office, Washington, 24 March 1965, FO 371/179788, PRO.
66. Memorandum, Minister of State's Visit to the Persian Gulf, 9–16 May 1965, FO 371/179790, PRO.
67. Telegram 202, Luce to Foreign Office, Bahrain, 18 March 1965, FO 371/179788, PRO.
68. Telegram 49, Tripp to Foreign Office, Bahrain, 29 March 1965, FO 371/179788, PRO.
69. Letter, Tripp to Weir, Bahrain, 14 June 1965, FO 371/179790, PRO.
70. Telegram 220, Luce to Foreign Office, Bahrain, 24 March 1965, FO 371/179791, PRO.
71. Telegram 219, Luce to Foreign Office, London, 24 March 1965, FO 371/179791, PRO.
72. Telegram 419, Foreign Office to Tehran, London, FO 371/179788, PRO.
73. Telegram 29, Tripp to Foreign Office, Bahrain, 15 March 1965, FO 371/179788, PRO.
74. Margaret Luce, *From Aden to the Gulf: Personal Diaries, 1956–1966* (London: Michael Russell, 1987), pp. 185–6.
75. Ibid., p. 187.
76. Memorandum, Tripp, Bahrain, 1 June 1965, FO 371/179791, PRO.
77. Telegram 44, Tripp to Foreign Office, Bahrain, 24 March 1965, FO 371/179788, PRO.
78. Telegram 40, Tripp to Foreign Office, Bahrain, 21 March 1965, FO 371/179788, PRO.
79. Letter, Brenchley to Luce, London, 21 May 1965, FO 371/179790, PRO.
80. Letter, Tripp to Weir, Bahrain, 14 June 1965, FO 371/179790, PRO.
81. Letter, Oldfield to Weir, Bahrain, 16 August 1965, FO 371/179790, PRO.
82. Letter, Political Agency to Weir, Bahrain, 2 October 1965, FO 371/179790, PRO.

83. Memorandum, First Impressions of Bahrain, Persian Gulf, 3 December 1965, FO 371/179790, PRO.
84. Lawson, *Bahrain: The Modernization of Autocracy*, p. 69.
85. Memorandum, First Impressions of Bahrain, Persian Gulf, 3 December 1965, FO 371/179790, PRO.
86. Anthony Parsons, *They Say the Lion: Britain's Legacy to the Arabs. A Personal Memoir* (London: Jonathan Cape, 1986), p. 124
87. Lawson, *Bahrain: The Modernization of Autocracy*, p. 97.
88. Parsons, *They Say the Lion*, 1986, p. 124.
89. Letter, Parsons to Luce, Bahrain, 14 March 1966, FO 371/185332, PRO.
90. Letter, Luce to Brenchley, Bahrain, 18 March 1966, FO 371/185332
91. Quoted in Rumaihi, *Bahrain: Social and Political Change since the First World War*, p. 304.
92. Letter, Parsons to Weir, Bahrain, 9 May 1966, FO 371/185328, PRO.
93. Anglo-Bahraini Talks, London, 2 June 1966, FO 371/185332, PRO.
94. Molly Izzard, *The Gulf* (London: John Murray, 1979), pp. 108–9.
95. Letter, Parsons to Weir, Bahrain, 11 July 1966, FO 371/185328, PRO.
96. Record of a Conversation, London, 8 November 1966, FO 371/185332, PRO.
97. Talking Points, Brief, 2a, London, 8 November 1966, FO 371/185332, PRO.
98. Letter, Parsons to Balfour-Paul, Bahrain, 4 October 1966, FO 371/185328, PRO.
99. Letter, Parsons to Balfour-Paul, Bahrain, 10 November 1966, FO 371/185328, PRO.
100. Hamad bin Isa Al Khalifa, *First Light: Modern Bahrain and its Heritage* (London: Kegan, 1994), p. 81.
101. *The Times* (London), 8 March 1999, p. 23.
102. Parsons, *They Say the Lion*, pp. 129-131.
103. Letter, Stewart to Brown, Arabia, 28 June 1967, FCO 8/44, PRO.
104. Letter, Crawford to Weir, Bahrain, 10 August 1967, FCO 8/44, PRO.
105. Lawson, *Bahrain: The Modernization of Autocracy*, p. 99.
106. Minute, Weir, London, 20 September 1967, FCO 8/114, PRO.
107. Minute, Vallat, London, 17 August 1967, FCO 8/108, PRO.
108. Memorandum of a Conversation, Bahrain, 1 November 1967, FCO 8/144, PRO.
109. Ibid.

4

Kuwait

In contrast to the Trucial States Qatar and Bahrain, in 1960, Kuwait, bordering Saudi Arabia on the south and Iraq on the north, was vigorously preparing for independence. In November 1960, a British officer visiting Kuwait called the country 'phenomenal' and the ruling Al Sabah family 'on the ball.' He was impressed with the shaikhdom's first-class buildings, roads, and water distillation plants. He admired the availability to Kuwaitis of free education and healthcare, but also noted that there were abundant signs of vulgarity. Among Shaikh Abdullah Mubarak's fleet of cars he saw a Cadillac trimmed with solid gold rather than chromium.[1]

Despite what was sometimes perceived as the lack of taste displayed by several members of the ruling Al Sabah family, since the availability of oil wealth after World War II, Kuwait had been transformed. In 1960, the small state on the northeastern shore of the Arabian Peninsula was preparing to emerge from under the protection of HMG, which had protected the shaikhdom since 1899. Although Kuwait and Britain accepted the necessity of adjusting their relationship, each continued to need the other. Kuwait was the source of approximately one-third of Britain's petroleum, and Kuwaiti investments in Britain were substantial. At the beginning of 1961, Kuwaiti ruler Shaikh Abdalla Salim Al Sabah asked for frank discussions with HMG. Discussions focused on how to advance independence but at the same time preserve Kuwait's special relationship with Britain.[2]

At the end of January, Lord Privy Seal Edward Heath paid a visit to Kuwait. The ruler provided an airplane for the British minister and his party explaining that he wanted his guests to see how the country had developed. Shaikh Abdalla Salim told Heath that Britain had been of considerable assistance to the shaikhdom and shared some credit for the material progress of his territory. Heath responded that Britain would always be prepared to help Kuwait, 'as far as she could.'[3]

Discussions between Britain and Kuwait moved forward and Washington requested information about the status of Kuwait's political evolution. The Foreign Office wanted the State Department to understand that 'we are not unwilling sanctioners of Kuwait's acquisition of independence.' According to London, full independence for Kuwait was logical and indicated the successful conclusion of British protection. 'Soon the only relic of our earlier position is likely to be a straightforward obligation to extend military protection...'[4]

The State Department indicated that Washington was confident that the British best understood the appropriate pace that political evolution in the Gulf States ought to take. The British Embassy in Washington reported that the Americans 'accept our judgment and disclaim any desire to question whether the pace adopted is too slow or too fast.' Such American approval had been unexpected and some British officials speculated that it sounded too good to be true.[5]

To complete arrangements for Kuwait's independence, the British suggested an exchange of letters, but on 19 April Shaikh Abdalla Salim instead presented a draft agreement to Political Resident Sir William Luce. The Political Resident explained that if Kuwait and Britain decided to conclude a treaty rather than simply to exchange letters, Parliament would be required to ratify that treaty before it took effect. However, if an exchange of letters would suffice, that information would simply be presented to Parliament and immediately become policy. Quickly the ruler opted for an exchange of letters.[6]

Meanwhile, as Kuwait prepared for independence, the shaikhs sought suitable candidates to train for their new diplomatic service. Shaikh Abdalla Salim wished 'to let by-gones be by gone,' and was willing to accept candidates who had earlier participated in a reform movement, which advocated curbing Al Sabah power. The Political Agency in Kuwait approved, stating: 'Kuwait can ill afford to deprive herself of any energy and abilities possessed by former Kuwaiti reformists.'[7]

Following the conclusion of negotiations, on 16 June 1961, the exchange of letters took place. In addition to independence, Kuwait received a guarantee of military support. This guarantee was to remain in force until abrogated by either party with three years' notice.[8] Ignoring very hot weather, joyous Kuwaitis celebrated their independence. Crowds gathered in the streets carrying Kuwaiti flags and pictures of the ruler, Amir Abdalla Salim Al Sabah.[9] At the same time, King Saud despatched two family members to call on Shaikh Abdalla Salim and extend best wishes. Most neighboring countries, including the UAR, sent messages of congratulations. Unfortunately, Iraqi President Abdul Karim Qasim was a 'glaring exception.'[10]

Sadly, Kuwaitis had little opportunity to savor their new independence before neighboring Iraq threatened to seize the amirate. The Iraqi dictator Qasim sent a telegram to Kuwait, the text of which was published in the Iraqi press. According to Qasim:

> I learned with pleasure that the British on 19 June 1961, acknowledged the abrogation of the illegal, forged and internationally unrecognized agreement which they called the 1899 agreement, and which they had illegally concluded with Sheikh Mubark Sabah – the then Governor of Kuwait annexed to Basrah District – without the knowledge of his brothers in Kuwait or legal authorities in Iraq at that time.[11]

British intelligence reported that Qasim's troops in southern Iraq were prepared to invade Kuwait and estimated that only a large force on the ground could repel the Iraqis. On the morning of 1 July, British marine commandos landed off Kuwait. Representing Kuwait at the United Nations, on 5 July, Abdul Aziz Hussein told the Security Council that although Kuwait did not want foreign troops on its soil, unfortunately, at present they were essential. Fifteen days later, on 20 July, Kuwait was admitted to the Arab League. Concerned with Arab opinion, the ruler moved quickly to invite an Arab League force to replace British troops. Political Resident Luce was uncertain that such a force would materialize and considered it vital to form a Kuwaiti army that in future would be strong enough to protect the state. Despite speculation that Arab League troops would not arrive, by the middle of September an Arab force was in place and British troops departed. It was clear, however, that if necessary Her Majesty's forces would quickly return.[12]

The British agreement to protect Kuwait permitted the Al Sabahs a measure of security that Arab League forces did not guarantee. Nasser soon decided to withdraw his forces from Kuwait, claiming that imperialist elements were spreading discord among the men from Arab League countries serving in Kuwait. However, the British were convinced that the reason the Egyptian leader withdrew his troops was that Amir Abdalla Salim had publicly reiterated his dependence on Britain.[13]

After independence, Kuwait's shaikhs decided to grant citizenship – a designation that did not consider tribal affiliation – only to those who had lived in the country since 1920. 'Citizenship was introduced as a new concept for the local Arabs, one largely of western origin and connected with the idea of the nation-state.'[14] More than one half of Kuwait's population was composed of workers who were ineligible for citizenship, and Kuwaiti leaders made no serious effort to ease restrictions on its acquisition. However, at the end of June the Amir appeared to recognize the contribution of a token number of expatriates, some in the highest level of his civil service. He published a decree on 25 June granting Kuwaiti nationality to 32 aliens. Among these new Kuwaitis were eleven Palestinians.[15]

After independence the Al Sabah shaikhs remained firmly in control and often were unwilling or unable to coordinate their activities. Defense was an urgent matter, but, alas, even in this critical area no proper system of management was introduced. Each shaikh ordered the military equipment that struck his fancy without reference to how his selected torpedo boat, rifle or grenades might fit it. One British official remarked:

> Qasim's folly has drawn Kuwait more quickly into international life than we had hoped and if she is to meet the responsibilities of independence we must bring home to the Sabah the dangers of unco-ordinated and ill-considered individual action, and the need for central decision making.[16]

Although lack of central direction remained a problem, the Al Sabah shaikhs moved to exercise their new independence. An announcement published in the *Official Gazette* on 20 August 1961 proclaimed that the head of state be given the title Amir of the State of Kuwait. At the same time, the Kuwaiti government requested that British titles, earlier awarded to the Amir, be omitted when addressing him. The request was 'in no sense a sign of disrespect, but an attempt to avoid preventing a target for the attacks of those who deny Kuwait's independent status.'[17]

Meeting at the Foreign Office at the end of August to discuss Britain's continuing role in the Gulf, Sir William Luce stated that British intervention in Kuwait had enhanced British influence in the region. His colleague, Deputy Under-Secretary of State Sir Roger Stevens, said that the Gulf was 'almost the only place left in the world' where Britain could act without the United States and other allies. He cautioned, however, that if Britain left the Gulf, neither the United States nor any other ally would take over. Sir William agreed that British withdrawal from the Gulf would leave a vacuum. It would lead to a struggle for power that would produce instability in the region and have a serious effect on the oil companies.[18]

Kuwaiti officials, too, speculated about the future. Among the Al Sabahs' major concerns was to ensure Kuwait's membership within the community of Arab states. In August the Kuwaiti government published a pamphlet that emphasized the country's support for Arab unity and, excluding Iraq, warmly praised Arab states. In addition, the pamphlet fervently thanked the Arab League states for their support.[19]

Returning to Kuwait after an absence of three months, the former Political Agent, later Consul General and now Britain's first Ambassador to Kuwait, John Richmond, described some of the changes he observed. 'Many of the few competent men available' had left to serve as diplomats in posts abroad. Richmond lamented the shortage of talent. Earlier he had hoped that the Iraqi threat would provide such a traumatic experience that the existing population would come together and develop a national consciousness. This had not happened. Most Kuwaiti citizens remained far removed from the expatriates who worked among them.[20]

Kuwaitis, of course, understood that alone they could not build their country; outsiders were essential. For example, a larger army was vital. By the end of 1961, three thousand new recruits had joined the Kuwaiti military. Most of these men came from Bedouin tribes which passed through Kuwaiti territory. Shaikhs, who resided in Kuwait from branches of these tribes, vouched for their loyalty. Ambassador Richmond speculated that within a year Kuwait might have a force capable of dealing with an Iraqi attack long enough to make successful British intervention possible.[21]

Given the great demand for workers in Kuwait, the appropriate role for Kuwaiti women was also considered. In December 1961, the Joint Council decided that women might be employed in the government departments of Social Affairs, Health, and Education, but were not to be hired in any other department, including the Ministry of Foreign Affairs. The newspaper *Al-Hadaf* opposed the decision to exclude women and began a campaign to have it reversed. Under pressure, the Joint Council announced that the women already employed by departments other than Social Affairs, Health and Education might remain at their jobs, but no new female employees would be hired. 'This only increased *Al-Hadaf*'s fury.' Meanwhile, another newspaper, *Al-Rai Al-Am*, told Kuwaiti women: 'be patient girls, work hard and show by your abilities that you are ready for emancipation.'[22]

Elections to Kuwait's Constituent Assembly of 20 members were held on 30 December 1961. Although this was the first election in

Kuwait's history, apathy prevailed. Only 40 percent of eligible Kuwaitis had registered to vote: 11,400 males. The British Embassy reported that the results indicated victory for 'more nonentities than we had expected and this perhaps indicates that the lower class of town Kuwaitis and the Bedu registered, at any rate in the suburban constituencies, in greater numbers than the merchants and businessmen.'[23] Among those elected was an outspoken leader of the reform movement, Dr Ahmed Khatib. Educated at the American University in Beirut, Khatib had been among the founders of the Arab National Movement and after his return to Kuwait had organized a local branch. In 1956, Khatib's activities in support of President Nasser of Egypt had led to an official warning that his duty was to treat patients, that if he continued to interfere in politics he would be imprisoned.[24]

At the beginning of January, Kuwait's government published an interim constitution, 'the latest incident in the Amirate's breathless adventure in democracy.' The constitution addressed the rights of the individual, declaring that 'Kuwaitis shall be equal before the Law.' British Ambassador Richmond called that sentence 'ominous.' Expatriates composed a majority of the population yet there was no provision for their protection.[25] Nevertheless, Richmond was favorably impressed with a provision of the interim constitution, which gave every assembly member the right to question any minister about the work of his ministry and mandated that the minister reply within one week. 'This is perhaps the most revolutionary provision in the whole document, and the most likely to attract the interest of the Kuwaitis, amongst whom reformism usually takes the form of complaints of inefficiencies and extravagances in the Departments rather than attacks on the Shaikhly system itself.' Richmond stated that if Dr Khatib was truly 'the fearless reformer that he is reputed to be,' that article provided him with the opportunity to question the management of every shaikh in charge of a government department.[26]

Kuwait's Foreign Minister, heir apparent Shaikh Sabah Al Salim Al Sabah, visited London in January 1963. He told Foreign Office officials that sometimes it might appear that both he and Amir Abdalla Salim were ignoring the British Ambassador in Kuwait, but that was not the case. In order to prevent attacks from other Arab states, the Al Sabahs had to avoid giving the impression that they paid too much attention to British officials, but he, like the Amir, regarded Britain as 'their best and truest friend.'[27] During the course of his stay in London, Shaikh Sabah Al Salim continued to praise the British, even comparing them to the sun. According to the visiting shaikh, 'There were some people who got too scorched by it, but clever people like the Kuwaitis knew how to take advantage of it without getting burnt.'[28]

Some British officials now expressed admiration for the Kuwaiti leadership and wanted Kuwait to serve as an example for the southern Gulf shaikhdoms. In the framework of their shaikhly regime, the Al Sabahs had successfully handled problems of administrative, legal, and judicial reform 'with remarkable skill.'[29] Earlier, one Foreign Office official had remarked that Kuwait's rulers attempted within a year or two to broaden its regime in a manner that in England took a century.[30] On 23 January 1963, as provided for in Kuwait's new Constitution, election of a fifty-member National Assembly took place. Two hundred and ten candidates sought seats. 'Because of the lack of political parties the candidates did not represent clear-cut platforms as is often the case in many democratic countries. However, the political ideologies of the candidates were not too ambiguous.'[31]

It was in Britain's interest, of course, that new ideas arrived in the Gulf from Kuwait rather than from Cairo. Hence, Whitehall suggested that in association with representatives of HMG, arrangements be made to provide Kuwaiti expertise to the amirate's neighbors. Among the suggestions put forward were that after the opening of the proposed university in Kuwait, students from other shaikhdoms should receive their higher education there. The Foreign Office also suggested that since soccer was popular in the Gulf region Kuwait might establish an Arabian Gulf Cup. In addition, London wanted Kuwaiti newspapers and television programs made available throughout the Gulf.[32]

In May 1963, after a protracted struggle, Kuwait was admitted to the United Nations. The Amir expressed gratitude to HMG for its assistance in helping the amirate achieve admission. At a press conference in New York in June 1961, an Iraqi representative had declared that Kuwait was not an independent state and, therefore, not eligible for membership in the United Nations.[33]

Initially siding with Iraq, the Soviet Union had refused to recognize Kuwaiti independence and, in November 1961, had vetoed Kuwait's application for United Nations membership. Again at the beginning of 1963, the Soviet Union continued its refusal to permit Kuwait entry. Amir Abdalla Salim wrote to Premier Nikita Khruschev, but received no reply.[34]

Then, on 8 February 1963, the situation changed after Iraqi dictator Qasim was killed during a coup which toppled his government. Kuwaitis were now optimistic that relations between the amirate and Iraq would improve and that the Soviet Union would extend recognition. Shortly after the demise of Qasim, Kuwaiti Permanent Observer at the United Nations, Abdur Razzaq Razzuqi, had discussed how to achieve admission with members of the British Mission to the United Nations. Razzuqi was soon to leave New York for Kuwait and possibly another assignment. Head of Chancery at Britain's United Nations Mission in New York, Alan Hugh Campbell, suggested that London impress upon the Al Sabahs the importance of maintaining an efficient staff in New York. 'It is not at all in their own interests to keep chopping and changing their staff. It is inefficient and makes them no more competent than some of the minor African delegations.'[35]

Throughout the process, British officials insisted that if HMG took too prominent a role in promoting Kuwait's candidacy for United Nations membership the result might damage Kuwait. Kuwaitis had to convince their Arab brothers, including Morocco, serving a term on the Security Council, to lend support. British officials had discussed the issue with the Moroccan representative to the United Nations, who claimed that the Arabs would resolve the problem themselves.[36]

In March 1963, there were indications of improving Iraqi–Kuwaiti relations. The Amir informed Ambassador John Richmond that traffic was moving between Basra and Kuwait, and that Kuwaiti travelers were kindly received. Shaikh Abdalla Salim hoped that it was now possible to obtain both Iraqi recognition and United Nations admission. He was willing to be patient and wanted the Arab League 'to carry the ball.'[37]

Despite the fall of Qasim, negotiations to achieve agreement on Kuwaiti admission to the United Nations continued to be difficult. In early May, the Arab states pressured Kuwaiti representatives to postpone the amirate's application. Only Saudi Arabia actively supported immediate Kuwaiti admission. Referring to the Amir, on 3 May the Kuwaiti Chargé in New York told Britain's Permanent Representative to the United Nations Sir Patrick Dean, 'out of deference to the representations made to him by the Arabs, he is prepared to wait for about forty-eight hours to see if this matter can still be resolved amicably.' Sir Patrick was certain that once the resolution to admit Kuwait was before the Council it would be difficult for members who already had diplomatic relations with the amirate to oppose Kuwait's membership. Since Morocco now refused to sponsor Kuwait, the amirate once again turned to Britain.[38]

After his country's admission to the United Nations, Shaikh Sabah stopped in London en route home from New York. He said that he had no illusions that the United Nations could help Kuwait, but he considered membership important in so far as it demonstrated that Kuwait was an independent state.[39] Now it appeared to both London and Kuwait that Iraqi recognition of the amirate had to be achieved. The British Foreign Office considered it unlikely that, as yet, Iraq would be willing to formally accept Kuwait's independence. However, Sir John Richmond suggested that 'if the Iraqi financial position is really desperate the Kuwaitis may now have a chance of squeezing recognition out of them without paying anything but money for it.'[40]

In return for recognition, Baghdad continued to press Kuwait for a substantial benefits package, including a large interest-free loan. Amir Abdalla Salim called a special session of the National Assembly to consider the Iraqi demand. The vote was not unanimous, but the assembly voted approval. Agreement between Kuwait and Iraq was announced on 4 October 1963. According to Ambassador Gordon Noel Jackson, 'there is a general feeling that Kuwait has been put in the undignified position of having to pay for something which most countries get free.'[41]

After Kuwaiti independence the British closely monitored communist activity in the amirate. The first Soviet Ambassador to Kuwait presented his credentials in August 1963. The amirate also established diplomatic relations with Czechoslovakia, Poland, and Bulgaria. And although Kuwait had diplomatic relations with Taiwan, in February 1964 the ruler told British officials that he supported the admission of Communist China to the United Nations. Whitehall noted that the Al Sabahs wanted a foot in both camps. The Kuwaitis 'no doubt reason that the best way to win friends and influence people is to be friendly themselves, and also that their emergence on the international stage can best be consolidated by a show of interest even in issues which do not directly concern them.' As a result, West German diplomats in the amirate expressed apprehension that Kuwait might follow its two-China policy with a two-German policy. The Foreign Office concluded that Britain could not prevent Kuwait's 'open-door' policy, but could minimize the damage by educating Kuwaiti officials about Communist methods.[42]

At the beginning of 1964, it appeared that Russian Embassy officials were actively courting Kuwait's Indian community, a community large enough to absorb troublemakers planted by the Communist Party. With the exception of a few wealthy merchants, most of the Indians living in Kuwait were 'in the underdog range,' working in low-level jobs. Because they had no ties to the regime, these Indians were likely targets of Soviet propaganda.[43] Soviet diplomats in Kuwait also used every opportunity to enhance their relationship with the amirate. In February 1964, the Soviet Ambassador to Kuwait told General Mubark that his government would be happy to supply the Kuwaitis with equipment and weapons. The Kuwaiti officer declined the offer. However, several days later, General Mubark received seven films pertaining to weapons: films that he had not requested. The films and the literature that accompanied them were in Russian. General Mubark regarded the episode as amusing. His British friends did not. They warned that if the Kuwaiti officer was not careful a Russian interpreter would soon be on his doorstep. General Mubark now promised that he would be cautious when dealing with Soviet representatives.[44]

British officials continued carefully to note even the most trivial indication of Soviet influence. During a national celebration, approximately ten thousand Kuwaiti students participated in a lavish gymnastics display organized by Egyptian teachers. Referring to the program as a display following the totalitarian pattern, an observer commented, 'The Kuwaitis seemed to be quite ignorant of the origins of this type of mass display and would hardly approve if they realised its associations.'[45]

Confident that it would serve London's interest if Kuwait established closer contacts with the British-protected neighboring Gulf States, in 1965, Ambassador Jackson suggested to Political Resident Luce that Kuwait and Bahrain be encouraged to exchange 'unofficial' representatives. According to Jackson, a Gulf Arab representing his own government would be in a position to help counter Egyptian and Arab League pressure on the amirate.[46] But the rulers of Bahrain were not interested. Bahrain's shaikhs were dissatisfied with what they considered to be Kuwait's patronizing attitude. In addition, there was no Bahraini of the caliber needed who could be spared for the assignment.[47]

In November 1965, Britain's friend and Kuwait's first amir, 73-year-old Shaikh Abdalla Salim Al Sabah, died. His successor, Shaikh Sabah Salim, was sworn in before the National Assembly. Commenting on the late Kuwaiti ruler, Ambassador Jackson praised Abdalla Salim's restraint for not having spent huge sums on himself, but according to Jackson:

Some members of his family and many of the businessmen of Kuwait, have accumulated immense undeserved fortunes and show no signs of trying to use them constructively: and more seriously, the welfare state in Kuwait, of which Abdulla Salim was the chief architect, has through its combination of free non-technical education, extensive employment opportunities in unproductive government service, and subsidized facilities of all kinds, made the average Kuwaiti something of a parasite without much ability to stand on his own feet in a competitive world.[48]

Together with several Conservative Members of Parliament, leader of Britain's Conservative Party Edward Heath visited Kuwait in January 1966. Heath asked to meet with the Amir. Keen not to appear to give 'any impression of cold-shouldering' the party out of power, Ambassador Jackson arranged meetings with both the ruler and the Prime Minister. The Conservative leader congratulated the Amir on his accession and on Kuwait's progress. He expressed pleasure that throughout 1965 Kuwait had continued to hold sterling and thanked the ruler for his confidence in Britain. The ruler declared that he was satisfied with the return on sterling investments and his British managers. The Ruler also said that relations with Britain were so very close and cordial that, when necessary, each could criticize the other without danger of offense.[49]

While the leader of Her Majesty's opposition met with Kuwaiti officials, Consul General Christopher Gandy took the British journalists who had accompanied Heath on a tour. The British Consul General pointed out the new hospitals, schools, and other public buildings that were a source of Kuwaiti pride. But the journalists appeared disinterested. They only wanted to photograph Arabs and camels.[50]

In October 1966, yet another Conservative leader, Reginald Maudling, met with the Amir and a group of Kuwaitis. Maudling asked the ruler for his impression of HMG's policy in the region. The Amir replied 'that it was not for him to give the Deputy Leader of the Opposition a handful of stones to throw at the Government.' Amir Sabah said that Britain was fortunate to have a loyal opposition, rather than an opposition that accepted direction from a foreign government. Jackson reported to the Foreign Office that this was the first occasion he had heard the ruler imply that some members of Kuwait's assembly, who had earlier resigned, took direction from the Egyptian Embassy, 'although we had known for a long time that they did so.'[51]

As Edward Heath had done earlier, Maudling also discussed sterling. He insisted that devaluation was 'out of the question.'

According to Maudling, devaluation would not solve Britain's financial problems; 'it would be political suicide for the Labour Party and most of the world's central banks opposed the idea.' Heir apparent, Prime Minister Shaikh Jabir Al Ahmed, said that, for the present, he was satisfied, but there was the danger that despite Britain's best intentions to make its financial policy work, it might not, and HMG would be forced to devalue.[52]

Meanwhile, British Army officers and Royal Air Force commanders stationed in Bahrain continued their practice of regular visits to Kuwait, where they called on General Mubark to discuss issues of mutual interest and to dispense advice. In June 1966, Kuwait was in the process of setting up its navy. Therefore, the British decided to include naval officers on such visits.[53]

Throughout 1966, security remained a major concern as incidents continued to take place on the Kuwaiti–Iraqi border. As Britain considered withdrawal from Aden, HMG retained its commitment to defend Kuwait, but changed the terms of that agreement. Taking effect on 1 February 1967, an 'air only' plan was introduced. Within one hour of agreeing to render assistance, a squadron from Bahrain would begin daylight patrols over Kuwaiti towns and along the Iraqi frontier. Within twenty-four hours additional squadrons would be available. The plan called for two states of alert, the first to be authorized by the Political Resident, the second declared by ministers.[54]

Yet another incident occurred on the Iraqi–Kuwaiti border on 18 April 1967. Escorted by armored cars, a group of Iraqis crossed the border and removed two Kuwaiti tents, which, although unoccupied, had earlier been used for passport examination. The next morning Iraqi planes flew three sorties over Kuwaiti territory.[55] The Amir did not appear to be overly concerned by Iraq's action. Later, Kuwaitis replaced the tents without any sign of Iraqi interference.

In April 1967, prior to the departure from London of the newly appointed British Ambassador to Kuwait, Geoffrey Arthur, the Foreign Office reviewed Kuwait's importance to Britain. Kuwait was a source of cheap crude oil, and, most important, had vast sterling holdings. A Foreign Office minute prepared for the Secretary of State stated that Kuwaitis wished for close links with the neighboring shaikhdoms still under British protection. But although Kuwait provided some assistance to these states, the aid given was always on Kuwaiti terms without appropriate consultation with local authorities. In addition, other Gulf rulers 'looked askance' at Kuwait's attempts to assume a leadership role.[56]

Two months later, as attention throughout the Gulf focused on the Arab–Israeli conflict, Kuwait, too, was deeply distressed by Israel's resounding victory. In August, the new British Ambassador evaluated the impact of the Six-Day War on Kuwait's relations with Britain. Arthur assumed that as a result of Egyptian propaganda, which claimed that British and American troops had assisted Israel, the war had done permanent damage to Britain's standing in Kuwait. 'Some of our former friends are now our enemies; many have become reserved and suspicious, ready to believe the worst of us; and even those who remain our friends have been badly shaken.'[57]

Ambassador Arthur asserted that the Arab defeat had undermined Kuwaiti confidence. The educated Kuwaiti

> has lost confidence in himself as well as in us, and this he can not forget. His shame, rather than his hatred, has come between us; and I suspect that the shame and frustration will remain, especially if Israel retains her conquests, when what hatred there is has passed. The shock has gone deep, and its effects are masked to some extent at present; but they must work themselves out in the end. I do not think that our position in Kuwait will ever again be quite what it was before the 5th of June, 1967.[58]

However, the British Ambassador also recognized that Kuwaitis continued to rely on the 1961 exchange of letters; that when Kuwaitis experienced pangs of insecurity, the government considered Britain's willingness to despatch military assistance reassuring. Ambassador Arthur also noted that while Kuwaitis continued to profess devotion to the Arab soil of Palestine, 'they are doing their utmost to avoid a further influx of troublesome Palestinians.'[59]

In November 1967, Minister of State for Foreign Affairs Goronwy Roberts met in Kuwait with the Amir and various officials, including the managing director of Kuwait Oil Company. During a meeting with Prime Minister Jabir Al Ahmed, Roberts emphasized Britain's commitment to remain in the region. Shaikh Jabir suggested that Britain ought to encourage the development of national forces in the area and promote an association of the Gulf States. According to the Kuwaiti Prime Minister, it was essential for the British to follow the wishes of the people of the Gulf rather than to impose their own plan. Roberts insisted that was, indeed, what London was trying to do: to convince the Gulf rulers to settle their numerous boundary disputes and to cooperate with one another. Roberts pointed to some positive developments in education and health. Then Shaikh Jabir emphasized that, during discussions with Gulf rulers, British officials ought to promote the importance of sharing 'some of their power' with their people. Roberts agreed.[60] According to the British Ambassador in Kuwait, Shaikh Jabir was 'somewhat enigmatic,' less supportive of Kuwait's British connection than other Al Sabah family members; a Kuwaiti whose opinion 'would have drawn cheers' from Britain's Treasury and from other Whitehall departments, that dissented from the government's policy in the Gulf.[61]

During his visit to Kuwait, Roberts also held talks with the Minister of Interior and Defense Shaikh Sa'ad, whose eyes blazed as he told Roberts 'in an emotional voice' that the Arabs would never recognize Israel. Roberts insisted that, for settlement to be reached, both sides would have to make concessions. The Kuwaiti minister listened patiently, but from time to time mumbled 'that death was better than dishonour.' Discussing Israel's victory in the June 1967 war, Roberts said that poor maintenance of Egypt's military equipment and a shortage of spare parts had contributed to the defeat of the Egyptian Army. Roberts asked if the Kuwaiti Army had studied that war from the technical viewpoint. Shaikh Sa'ad was embarrassed by the question and Roberts immediately changed the subject; he said that he had heard that Kuwaiti soldiers 'had acquitted themselves very well last June.' Shaikh Sa'ad was delighted with Robert's remark and the two discussed the recruitment and training of the Kuwaiti military. Shaikh Sa'ad assured the British minister that, as long as it was provided at a reasonable price, Kuwait would continue to obtain all of its military equipment from Britain.[62] But Roberts' visit did not attract a great deal of publicity in Kuwait. The British Embassy had earlier decided not to hold a press conference, stating that the value of such a press conference was outweighed by the 'dangers of misrepresentation.'[63]

While Roberts visited Kuwait, British observers reported a considerable amount of anti-American feeling. One British official said that the 'emotional reaction of June has given way to a more deep-seated and reasoned hostility.' He had discussed his observation with American officials in the amirate. They had agreed, and suggested that it was likely that anti-American feeling had some official backing.[64]

Unlike the neighboring protected shaikhdoms, the Trucial States Qatar and Bahrain, by the end of 1967 Kuwait was an independent nation with membership in the Arab League and the United Nations. The Al Sabahs pursued their own foreign policy, often without consultations with London. Yet, the special relationship between

Britain and the amirate remained, for Kuwait was unable to safeguard its independence. Hence, the British commitment to protect Kuwait remained the cornerstone of Kuwait's security.

NOTES

1. Letter, McDermott to Stevens, Episkopi, 10 November 1960, FO 371/148919, PRO. An unsigned Foreign Office comment on the margin of the British visitor's letter declared, 'I would not have a Cadillac.'
2. Telegram 2, Richmond to Foreign Office, Kuwait, 2 January 1961, FO 371/156834, PRO.
3. Letter, Richmond to Middleton, Kuwait, 21 January 1961, FO 371/156834, PRO.
4. Letter, Walmsley to Weir, London, 3 March 1961, FO 371/156834, PRO.
5. Letter, Weir to Walmsley, Washington, 13 March 1961, FO 371/156834, PRO.
6. Meeting, Qasr As-sif, 19 April 1961, FO 371/156834, PRO.
7. Letter, Political Agency to Arabian Department, Kuwait, 11 March 1961, FO 371/156825, PRO.
8. Miriam Joyce, *Kuwait 1945–1996, An Anglo-American Perspective* (London: Frank Cass, 1998), p. 87.
9. Ibid., p. 94.
10. Telegram 260, Richmond to Foreign Office, 21 June 1961, FO 371/156836, PRO.
11. Quoted in Joyce, *Kuwait 1945–1996*, p.93.
12. Ibid., pp. 106-8.
13. Ibid., p. 109.
14. Andrzej Kapiszewski, *Nationals and Expatriates* (Reading, MA: Ithaca University Press, 2001), pp. 49–50.
15. Letter, Goulding to Hillier-Fory, Kuwait, 29 June 1961, FO 371/156825, PRO.
16. Letter, Black to Walmsley, Kuwait, 29 July 1961, FO 371/156825, PRO.
17. Letter, Consul General to Arabian Department, Kuwait, 20 August 1961, FO 371/156826, PRO.
18. Record of a Meeting, London, 24 August 1961, FO 371/1568377, PRO.
19. Letter, Consulate General to Arabian Department, Kuwait, 31 August 1961, FO 371/156842.
20. Letter, Richmond to the Earl of Home, 10 December 1961, Kuwait, FO 371/156826, PRO.
21. Ibid.
22. Letter, British Embassy to Arabian Department, Kuwait, 10 December 1961, FO 371/156825, PRO.
23. Letter, Chancery to Arabian Department, Kuwait, 31 December 1961, FO 371/162881, PRO.
24. Joyce, *Kuwait 1945–1996*, p. 34.
25. Letter, Richmond to the Earl of Home, Kuwait, 13 January 1962, FO 371/162881, PRO.
26. Ibid.
27. Minute, Walmsley, London, 3 January 1963, FO 371/168784, PRO.
28. Minute, Walmsley, London, 9 January 1963, FO 371/168784, PRO.
29. Minute, Gracie, London, 1 October 1963, FO 371/168624, PRO.
30. Minute, Walmsley, London, 9 January 1963, FO 371/168784, PRO.

31. Hassan A. Al-Ebraheem, *Kuwait: A Political Study* (Kuwait: Kuwait University Press, 1975), p. 138.
32. Minute, Gracie, London, 1 October 1963, FO 371/168624, PRO.
33. Telegram 1062, Dean to Foreign Office, New York, 28 June 1961, FO 371/156842.
34. Minute, Walmsley, London, 10 January 1963, FO 371/168746, PRO.
35. Letter, Campbell to Given, New York, 23 February 1963, FO 371/168746, PRO.
36. Ibid.
37. Letter, Richmond to Crawford, Kuwait, 3 March 1963, FO 371/168746, PRO.
38. Telegram 628, Dean to Foreign Office, New York, 2 May 1963, FO 371/168746, PRO.
39. Record of a Conversation, London, 23 May 1963, FO 371/168783, PRO.
40. Telegram 252, Richmond to Foreign Office, Kuwait, 16 May 1963, FO 371/168739, PRO.
41. Quoted in Joyce, *Kuwait 1945–1996*, p.133.
42. Minute, Black, London, 21 February 1964, FO 371/174585, PRO.
43. Letter, Errock to Snellgrove, Kuwait, 5 February 1964, FO 371/174585, PRO.
44. Letter, Errock to Snellgrove, Kuwait, 10 February 1964, FO 371/174585, PRO.
45. Letter, Battiscombe to Berthoud, Kuwait, 28 February 1966, FO 371/185443, PRO.
46. Letter, Jackson to Luce, Kuwait, 29 March 1965, FO 371/179793, PRO.
47. Letter, Berthoud to Rich, Bahrain, 14 June 1965, FO 371/179793, PRO.
48. Quoted in Joyce, *Kuwait 1945–1996*, p. 141.
49. Letter, Jackson to Brenchley, Kuwait, 17 January 1966, FO 371/185433, PRO.
50. Ibid.
51. Letter, Jackson to Brenchley, Kuwait, 29 October 1966, FO 371/185433, PRO.
52. Ibid.
53. Letter, Graham to Brenchley, Kuwait, 20 June 1966, FO 371/185433, PRO.
54. Minute, Foreign Office, London, 19 April 1967, FCO 8/628, PRO.
55. Telegram 124, Jackson to Foreign Office, Kuwait, 19 April 1967, FCO 8/627, PRO.
56. Minute, Weir, London, 25 April 1967, FCO 8/612, PRO.
57. Letter, Arthur to Brown, Kuwait, 20 August 1967, FCO 8/614, PRO.
58. Ibid.
59. Ibid.
60. Conversation, Kuwait, 8 November 1967, FCO 8/144, PRO.
61. Letter, Arthur to Brenchley, 12 November 1967, FCO 8/144, PRO.
62. Conversation, Kuwait, 9 November 1967, FCO 8/144, PRO.
63. Letter, Arthur to Brenchley, 12 November 1967, FCO 8/144, PRO.
64. Letter, Gordon to Ibbott, Kuwait, 12 November 1967, FCO 8/637, PRO.

5

Oman

In 1960, the Sultanate of Muscat and Oman was an independent state. Although not legally under British protection, the sultanate and Britain had very strong ties and the Sultan heavily relied on British assistance. HMG subsidized the Sultan's Armed Forces (SAF), where seconded and contract British officers served. In addition, the Sultan granted the RAF facilities in his territory and often, at the Sultan's request, Britain handled Muscat and Oman's foreign affairs. Unlike Bahrain, the sultanate had not yet had the benefit of even modest oil revenue. The cautious Sultan, therefore, steadfastly refused to permit development. Oman lacked schools, healthcare facilities, and roads.

Earlier, in 1954, leading the tribes of the interior of Oman, the Imam Ghalib bin Ali had claimed independence from the Sultan. Despite the 1920 Agreement of Sib, signed by the Political Agent in Muscat on behalf of the Sultan and the Imam of Oman, Mohammed bin Abdallah, tribal rivalries and conflict between the more cosmopolitan coast and the conservative interior had continued. The Agreement of Sib permitted local autonomy but did not recognize Oman as an entity separate from Muscat.[1] Thus, in 1954 the British provided military assistance to defeat the rebels and were initially successful. The Sultan permitted the deposed Imam to retire to a remote village. However, Ghalib's brother, Talib bin Ali, received aid from the Saudis who, as a result of a dispute over the area of Buraimi, were angry with the Sultan. During the summer of 1957, leading a rebel force, Talib and the leader of the Beni Riyam tribe, Suleiman bin Himyar, took control of central Oman. Once again the British came to the Sultan's rescue and the rebels retreated to the remote Jebel Akhdar massif, where they received encouragement from both Saudi Arabia and Egypt. With the assistance of the RAF and British officers seconded to the Sultan's forces, in 1959 the Sultan recovered the interior of Oman.[2] However, rebellion did not end and during the

1960s the Sultan was faced with constant rebel activity, particularly in the region of Dhofar, the southernmost portion of his country.

Nevertheless, in 1960 the sultanate experienced a period of relative tranquility. A British official traveling through the interior of Oman visited the ancient Ibadhi capital of Nizwa, where he described the people as calm and their *Wali* as melancholy. 'The Sultan's civil administration is tolerated because it has to be, but it seems at present to be regarded as more of an alien imposition than is the presence of the almost wholly foreign SAF.' The official also noted that the morale of the Sultan's Armed Forces was good and that 'the Pakistani NCO's are a tough lot; my superficial impression is that, despite their being Moslem, they are less liked by the local Omanis than are their Christian officers.' It appeared that Britain, not the Sultan, was credited with the small steps toward modernization that occurred in the region, and he advised that British officials attempt to identify the Sultan with any benefits his people received. He also advised that improved healthcare would pay the biggest dividend and that construction of a good road from Muscat to Nizwa ought to have top priority.[3]

In the spring of 1962, Egypt continued broadcasts directed against the Sultan. During many of these broadcasts, fantasy passed for news. While playing bridge in Muscat on 22 March, the Sultan's brother, Sayyid Tariq bin Taimour, told his British friends that the previous evening, as he listened to Cairo radio, he heard that following an unsuccessful coup he, Tariq, had fled Oman. But not all Arab nationalist efforts were devoted to propaganda. Mines were frequently laid in the sultanate, and explosions continued to kill people and livestock.[4]

While HMG steadfastly defended the Sultan, some Britons opposed to the policies of the Omani ruler publicly expressed their disapproval. A citizens' committee, chaired by Member of Parliament Judith Hart, asked the Foreign Office why the Sultan imprisoned political opponents without trial, why the Sultan did not permit the International Red Cross to aid Omani wounded, and why slavery continued to be permitted in the sultanate. Responding to these questions, the Arabian Department replied that it was, indeed, true that the Sultan imprisoned political opponents without trial, but that other rulers did the same. In addition, the Red Cross was not needed to tend wounded since war had ended. As far as concerned slavery, the Arabian Department explained that slavery was permitted by Islam and continued throughout Arabia, including in the sultanate. Yes, slaves served in the Sultan's household, but the Department emphasized that the Sultan had cooperated in ending the slave trade and that any slave who wished could obtain freedom by applying to the British Consulate.[5]

Meanwhile, intent on putting the rebellion behind him, the Sultan offered amnesty to Omanis now in Damman and in other locations outside of his territories, agreeing to their return provided that they pledged loyalty to him.[6] By March 1962 the SAF estimated that, under the amnesty, more than one hundred former rebels returned to Oman, seven of who were considered prominent men.[7] Nevertheless, several of the rebellion's former leaders remained in exile, where they continued to stir up trouble, among them the paramount chief of the Beni Riyam, Suleiman bin Himyar. Desiring reconciliation between Omani rebel leaders and the Sultan, the British wished to arrange an agreement between Shaikh Suleiman and the Sultan: an agreement that would permit the rebel leader to return home. The Omani ruler demurred. The Sultan claimed that Shaikh Suleiman had oppressed his own tribesmen and now they were happier without him. According to the Sultan, there was no place in the present or the future for a paramount Shaikh. Political Resident Sir William Luce told the Sultan that Shaikh Suleiman was no longer a young man. It appeared that he wished to live peacefully in his homeland. The Political Resident asked the Sultan to agree that after Shaikh Suleiman had spent five years in exile without involvement in any sort of subversive activity he would be permitted to return to Birkat al Mauz as Shaikh of his own section of the Beni Riyam. The Sultan had no objection if Suleiman wished to consider himself the Shaikh of his tribal section, the Nabhani, which merely indicated a small group of Suleiman's own relatives. However, the Sultan continued to distrust Shaikh Suleiman and refused to allow his return to Oman, nor was he now willing to consent to his return after five years.[8]

Unable to move the Sultan on the issue of Suleiman, the Political Resident asked the Omani ruler to consider releasing Suleiman's son, Sultan bin Suleiman, who was incarcerated in Jalali prison. The Sultan refused. He insisted that Sultan bin Suleiman was not a hostage but had been imprisoned for acts which he himself had committed. The only concession that the Sultan made was that, excluding Suleiman's imprisoned son, he agreed to permit other family members of Suleiman bin Himyar to join him in exile.[9]

Persuading the Sultan to accept British advice often failed. Kuwait's Amir Abdalla Salim told his British friends it was a pity that the Sultan did not take an active role in conducting relations with other Arabs. The Amir explained that British representations on behalf of the

Sultan were often counterproductive.[10] British officials attempted to convince the Sultan that it would be wise to employ his own subjects in key military and civil positions. Sultan Said disagreed. Since education was unavailable in the sultanate, the small number of his subjects who were educated had studied abroad where they acquired a foreign outlook and dangerous Arab nationalist ideas. The Sultan wished to continue employing foreigners, especially Englishmen, whom he considered to be trustworthy. Sultan Said claimed that Arabs, 'were always trying to play as an orchestra with ghastly results because they could not maintain harmony.' Given the Sultan's position, it appeared unlikely that, as long as he remained in power, the sultanate would acquire an indigenous civil and military administration. At the same time, it seemed likely that British subjects would remain in a variety of positions, both civil and military.[11]

As Shell Oil Company began drilling in 1962, British officials expected that funds from oil might bring improvements to the country. But Political Resident Luce told the Foreign Office:

> The Sultanate can not become viable, in any proper sense of the word, within the next ten years. The acquisition of substantial revenue from oil production would of course make the Sultanate financially independent, but it would still not solve the problem of creating indigenous and effective administration and security organizations.[12]

Basic differences in outlook between British officials and the Sultan extended to numerous issues. Britain wanted to present the sultanate as a country that was emerging from feudal society, but the Sultan appeared to have little concern about his image abroad. The Sultan of Oman wanted a quiet life, 'relying on Allah and the British.'[13]

Hoping to improve living conditions for the Sultan's subjects, in 1960 Britain had agreed to increase the subsidy that it paid to the sultanate. The British wanted to extend civil development, providing roads, schools, and healthcare. But by spring 1963 development was far behind schedule. Delay increased when the Sultan imposed a ban on all new projects until he could hire a suitable employee to fill the post of Development Secretary, a post that had been vacant for six months.[14]

The situation in Oman continued to be a matter of concern at the United Nations, where some countries considered the Sultan a 'British Stooge.' The British delegation in New York complained that it was difficult to defend the Sultan, who had the tendency to hide behind 'our coat-tails.' Members of other delegations suggested that an Omani represent the Sultan at the United Nations debates on the situation in his territories.[15] The Sultan was not interested. Nevertheless, as a result of British efforts, on 14 December 1962 a resolution sponsored by Arab states, calling for recognition of the independence of the people of Oman and the withdrawal of foreign forces from Oman, failed to secure the necessary two-thirds majority vote in the General Assembly.[16]

Although he refused to accept the right of the international body to discuss the internal affairs of the sultanate, in 1963 the Sultan invited a United Nations representative to visit Salalah. In May 1963, on behalf of the United Nations, Swedish diplomat Herbert de Ribbing met the Sultan and afterwards visited the Imam Ghalib bin Ali in Saudia Arabia. Nothing was resolved, but the United Nations continued to discuss Oman. Convinced that outsiders did not understand local conditions, the annoyed Sultan proclaimed that no Middle East leader would willingly allow the United Nations to meddle in his relations with his subjects.[17]

While HMG continued to defend the Sultan at the United Nations, British officials also considered how to defend the Sultan's son, Sayyid Qaboos, from his father's plan to keep him isolated. The young prince had attended Sandhurst and had also traveled in Europe. However, he had never seen the sultanate's capital, Muscat, which was five hundred miles across the desert from his home in Salalah. After Qaboos returned to the sultanate, his father did not permit him either to tour the country or to establish contact with the people. Instead, he was confined to Salalah, the Dhofari town that served as his father's residence. Sayyid Qaboos lived with a tutor who instructed him in the Koran. The Sultan's son had few companions, none with experience of life outside the sultanate. According to Margaret Luce, wife of Political Resident Sir William, Sayyid Qaboos truly enjoyed classical music, but the record player he had purchased in England did not work on Salalah's voltage so, in the spring of 1965, the isolated young prince patiently waited for a part to arrive.[18]

Sayyid Qaboos was not the only dissatisfied young Omani. Given the absence of opportunity in Dhofar, younger men, especially among the Bedu and the Jibali, sought employment abroad. Large numbers found work in Kuwait and Qatar. Returning home they were dissatisfied with the absence of development; they were no longer willing to obey their shaikhs or their fathers. Unsympathetic, the Sultan complained that these young men were 'like rats, coming out to bite the Government and run back quickly into their holes.'[19]

As discontent continued in the sultanate, events in Zanzibar created a momentary distraction. At the beginning of 1964, a revolution in Zanzibar led to the persecution of the Arab population of that African state which, until 1861, had been part of the Omani empire. Many of Zanzibar's Arabs had retained ties to Oman. Fearing for their safety, these Arabs left for the sultanate in any available vessel, from motor launches to dhows. Quickly, the Sultanate accepted 2,500 refugees and the International Red Cross, together with local merchants, provided food and shelter.[20]

Although the Sultan was willing to allow entry of Arab refugees from Zanzibar, he continued to be adamantly opposed to permitting the return of the tribal leaders who had rebelled against him. The Sultan's attitude toward these Omanis angered Saudi King Faisal, who wanted the British to reach an agreement with the exiled Omanis, including the leader, Imam Ghalib: an agreement that would permit the rebels to return to their homes. British official, Morgan Mann, now responded that it was unreasonable to expect the Sultan to hand over considerable territory to men who had rebelled against his rightful authority. The Saudi ruler warned that if the exiled Omanis were not allowed to return to their lands, they would seek help from Egypt, China, and Russia and remain a constant source of trouble. Mann told King Faisal that since these Omanis were now in Saudi Arabia he could curb their activities. King Faisal responded that he could not prevent them from traveling abroad. Then the Saudi monarch exploded, calling the Sultan 'a detestable and tyrannical usurper who had no right to any place but Muscat and who should really go home to where he belonged – India.'[21]

Rebel activity in the sultanate continued. In August 1965, the Wali of Dhofar warned of possible attack on the RAF airfield and camp located in Salalah. As a result, to assist in the defense of the targeted area the British government authorized the despatch of one platoon from Bahrain to Salalah.[22] While it now appeared that, despite his aversion to the Sultan, King Faisal was not providing active support for the rebels, it was clear that they continued to travel through Saudi territory toward Dhofar and that they carried supplies of arms and materials to utilize for sabotage.[23]

Neighboring rulers could not understand why Britain did not insist that the Sultan make peace with the rebels. In Kuwait, the head of the Amir's *Diwan* asked Ambassador Christopher Gandy why Britain did not just threaten the Sultan that HMG would withdraw its support. In December, Middle East expert Sir Alex Kirkbride visited the Sultan in

Salalah. According to Kirkbride, 'the longer the Sultan tries to keep a dam against the outside world the worse will be the crash when it falls.'[24]

Kuwaitis still wished to reach the Sultan. The Amir was willing to attempt mediation between Imam Ghalib and the Sultan, but Ambassador Noel Jackson told him that there was little chance of success. The Imam had numerous channels of approach to the Sultan but continued to demand unrealistic terms. According to Sultan Said, the Imam and his entourage were rebels who started a costly war. They were defeated and fled the country. There was no place for them in his territory.[25]

British officials continued their attempts to understand the Omani Sultan and to justify his policies. At the same time, of course, Her Majesty's officials looked to the best interests of their country. The British concluded that the return of Imam Ghalib was not a good idea, for the exiled leader was 'deeply committed to Cairo and Baghdad.'[26]

On 18 April 1966, the Middle East News Agency carried a report from the Dhofar Liberation Front stating that the Sultan of Oman had been wounded. British authorities failed to pick up the story, which later appeared to provide evidence that Cairo had advance knowledge of rebel plans. As yet, no attempt had been made on the Sultan's life.[27] Soon after, however, on 26 April 1966, some of the Sultan Said bin Taimour's soldiers, most from the indigenous non-Arab tribes who lived in the mountains, attempted to assassinate him. They failed. Although several involved in the plot were arrested, none were executed.[28]

During the entire ordeal the Sultan remained 'phenomenally calm.' The Pakistani Commander of the Dhofar Force, Lieutenant Colonel Mohammed Sakhi Raja, was severely wounded and one of his officers, Second Lieutenant Sattar Shah, later died of his wounds. The largest number of soldiers serving in the Dhofar Force came from the Khaddam, an area of plain adjacent to the sea. These men, descendants of African slaves, remained loyal to the Sultan and assisted Pakistani Adjutant-Captain Nur Mohammed to regain control over the barracks. When 45 men from the SAF arrived, they noted that order had already been restored; 22 Jibalis were imprisoned and 19 others ran away, presumably to join the rebels in the mountains. Now the British wanted the Sultan to disband the Dhofar Force. Confident in the loyalty of the Khaddam, the ruler said no, 'he might like to have a Dhofar Force to turn to if it was SAF's turn to mutiny next.'[29]

Later in Sharjah, British Resident in Bahrain Sir William Luce met with the Sultan's brother, Sayyid Tariq. After finally accepting the futility of his efforts to influence the Sultan to improve conditions in Oman, Sayyid Tariq had left the sultanate in November 1962. Now, Sir William asked Tariq if perhaps the attempted assassination might influence his brother to change. Tariq said no. He claimed that the Sultan was conceited; only concerned about not losing face.[30]

On 8 May 1966, British Consul General in Muscat Bill Carden visited Sayyid Qaboos in Salalah. Sayyid Qaboos, who rarely saw the Sultan, was concerned that yet another attempt on his father's life would be made, and that his father might not survive. The Sultan's son asked Carden what he ought to do if his father was killed. The British representative advised that if the Sultan was assassinated, Qaboos should surround himself with reliable servants who were ready and able to fight for him. In addition, Carden counseled that Qaboos immediately send for SAF troops, go to Muscat to obtain Al Bu Said recognition as Sultan and the allegiance of tribal leaders as well as the allegiance of the Wali of Oman. Carden also advised that Qaboos ought quickly to announce development programs in Oman and in Dhofar. Although he denied that he was criticizing his father, Sayyid Qaboos expressed regret that the Sultan had completely cut himself off from the Dhofari people. In earlier years, after the rains, together with their shaikhs the men of Dhofar came to visit their ruler and shared their problems with him. Sayyid Qaboos was dismayed that the present situation necessitated ruling Dhofar with the rifle.[31] In the course of his meeting with the British representative, Sayyid Qaboos also discussed Nasser. Both the Englishman and the Omani agreed that while the Egyptian leader had achieved some good for his people, 'it would be a blessing if he disappeared from the international stage and the sooner the better.'[32]

Political Resident in Bahrain Sir William Luce now considered assassination of the Sultan probable. He was concerned that, without an effective central government, Saudi and UAR elements would vie for control of Omani territory and the result would be chaos; a situation that would serve neither British interests nor the interest of the Shell Oil Company. Looking to the future, Luce considered Sayyid Tariq to be the most likely candidate to become Sultan. Meanwhile, Sayyid Tariq appeared to favor his nephew, Qaboos, and was extremely critical of both his brother and the British. The Sultan's brother, Tariq, wanted establishment of an Omani government that did not depend on the 'character or wisdom or stupidity' of one man.

He suggested that Britain force the Sultan to permit Sayyid Qaboos to take a role in the affairs of state. Meanwhile, Political Resident Luce was confident that if Tariq had power, he would turn to Saudia Arabia, rather than to Egypt, and thus take an important step in the direction of Arabian Peninsula solidarity.[33]

During 1966, rebellion against the Sultan intensified. British sources verified that the rebels had an Egyptian-supported base in Hauf, in the East Aden protectorate. Between June and September, four clashes between government troops and rebel forces occurred, including one that took place close to the RAF base. At the same time, two rebel groups attempted to coordinate their activities. They failed because, although both groups opposed Sultan Said, one, the Dhofar Liberation Front, wanted an independent Dhofar region, while most rebels favored a united state.[34]

Finally realizing the need to show some interest in the development of his shaikhdom, the Sultan asked that the London *Times* carry an announcement stating that he had commissioned the firm of John R. Harris, architects and planners, to undertake a large-scale development plan for the Muscat–Mutrah region. This plan included the design and construction of houses, schools, and hospitals. The BBC Arabic Service carried the announcement, generating a positive response from the Sultan's subjects.[35]

Meanwhile, concerned with fostering better relations among the Gulf rulers, in October 1966 Political Resident Glen Balfour-Paul encouraged Abu Dhabi's ruler, Shaikh Zaid, to hold discussions with the Sultan. Relations between the two states were generally good and Consul General in Muscat Carden suggested that a meeting between the two rulers might help bring the Sultan 'out of his shell.'[36] According to Balfour-Paul, it was unlikely that Sultan Said would leave Salalah and so Abu Dhabi's ruler would have to be willing to travel there.[37] As a result, Shaikh Zaid wrote to the Sultan suggesting a meeting. The Omani ruler expressed his gratitude and reviewed the long record of friendship between the two states, recalling that his grandfather, Shaikh Faisal Al Bu Said, had visited Abu Dhabi at the beginning of the twentieth century. Nevertheless, Sultan Said was not yet prepared to issue an invitation to Shaikh Zaid. Claiming that Muscat would be the appropriate place for such a meeting, he said that he would arrange it for the future. The Sultan also suggested that perhaps the two might be in London at the same time, and if so could meet there.[38]

The Sultan's brother, Sayyid Tariq, however, was happy to have the opportunity to visit Shaikh Zaid, and in November 1966 was in Abu Dhabi as the ruler's guest. Sayyid Tariq now wished to oust his brother and become regent for his nephew, Qaboos. Shaikh Zaid was unwilling to assist in an effort to depose Sultan Said. Although earlier he had been prepared to act against Sharjah's Shaikh Saqr bin Sultan, Shaikh Zaid would not move against the Sultan. Instead, Shaikh Zaid wanted to cooperate with the Sultan of Oman and wished to meet with him as soon as possible.[39]

As usual, the Sultan insisted on remaining in Salalah on the Indian Ocean, approximately midway between Aden and Muscat. Since no civilian aircraft had scheduled flights to Salalah, Sultan Said's address was c/o AOC, British Forces, Aden. Consul General Carden was concerned about international opinion. At the United Nations, the British claimed that Oman was not a colonial dependency, but the Sultan appeared to indicate otherwise. Carden wanted the Sultan's address changed, omitting all reference to Britain. However, the British diplomat admitted that the Sultan was far less concerned than he was.[40]

Sultan Said's refusal to leave Salalah unless he was traveling to London had earlier prompted a Saudi diplomat, Mohammed Rumaih, to declare that such isolation was a sin. According to Rumaih, the Sultan's refusal to receive visitors in his *majlis* and move among his own people was wrong. Rumaih predicted that once Sultan Said had oil money, even if he spent it wisely, he would be unable to 'win the hearts' of his subjects without establishing real contact with them.[41]

Political Resident Sir Stewart Crawford dined with the Sultan on 7 March 1967. The Sultan was considering a wife for his son, Qaboos, one from the Harth tribe. Meanwhile, he still refused to provide his son with any sort of employment. Further, the Sultan explained to the Political Resident that Qaboos did not necessarily have to be his successor. Reviewing the last three generations of his family, the Sultan remarked that his great-grandfather had seized power from another branch of the family, that his grandfather had been a second son. True, in the following two generations power had passed from father to son. Nevertheless, Sultan Said did not say one word about whom he wished to rule after him.

As dinner progressed, the Political Resident discussed the possibility of a meeting between the Sultan and King Faisal during the Sultan's planned visit to London. The Sultan rejected the idea, but said he wished 'when he could get away' to go to Mecca for the Haj. Perhaps in the future, while he was in Saudi Arabia, a meeting with King Faisal might be arranged.[42]

During Political Resident Crawford's visit, the Sultan also talked about the prisoners retained in Jalali, about 150 men. The Sultan insisted that conditions in the prison were improving and that he would release some of these prisoners if their families or shaikhs provided guarantees of good behavior. According to the Sultan, some families refused to provide such a guarantee, preferring their relative to remain in prison.[43]

At the end of April 1967, another of the Sultan's brothers, Sayyid Fahr bin Taimour, left the sultanate. Sayyid Fahr claimed that he would not return. Prior to his departure, Sayyid Fahr had administered motor transport and wireless communications. But like Sayyid Tariq, Fahr had lost patience with the Sultan's restrictions and his refusal to spend money. The British considered Fahr's departure a 'blow' to the Sultan. 'It will raise Tariq's standing on the Batinah in Muscat and Matrah and abroad.'[44]

During talks on 3 May with the chief representative of the Petroleum Development Company, the Sultan said that he was confident that he would remain in control. He admitted that some groups would continue efforts to oust him, but claimed that most of the important shaikhs were with him. He planned to develop agriculture, fisheries, and health. However, he had to pursue development slowly and avoid appearing to favor one or another group. Hence, he could not develop one area before he was able to provide the same amenities to all areas. Shortly afterwards, as Political Resident Crawford boarded a plane in Bahrain for a flight to London, he was surprised to meet both Sayyid Tariq and Sayyid Fahr. When Tariq left the aircraft for a brief stop in Kuwait, Sayyid Fahr and the Political Resident had a short visit. Sir Stewart reminded Fahr that oil production in Oman would begin in the autumn and the Sultan was already planning extensive development. The Political Resident said that the country had been waiting for development and that it would be 'absolutely tragic' if unrest inside the sultanate further delayed progress. Sayyid Fahr considered the Political Resident over-optimistic. He doubted that the Sultan would use his new wealth to improve conditions. Sir Stewart demurred. He was certain that Sultan Said was now willing to move forward. Sayyid Fahr appeared uncomfortable; gesturing towards his brother, Tariq, who had just returned to the aircraft, he said: 'I had better follow the fat old man.'[45]

At the beginning of July, Sayyid Fahr was residing in Dubai and British officials there considered him to be a problem. The Sultan's brother wanted employment in some official capacity. According to

Dubai's Political Agency, 'Fahr, whether we like it or not, is obviously going to be hanging around us in Dubai for some time.'[46] The British Consulate in Muscat did not deny that Sultan Said had treated his brothers 'shabbily.' Nevertheless, Muscat advised Dubai not to give in to sympathy, that a job for Fahr, who was so closely identified with Tariq, might indicate that HMG approved of the brothers' stand against the Sultan. At the same time, Muscat indicated that it was possible that Tariq and Fahr would part company because the latter was 'too jovial, talkative and indiscreet' to participate in the political movement that Tariq wanted to establish.[47]

During a visit to the Sultan in July 1967, Consul General Carden was pleased to learn that the Sultan had finally agreed to meet Shaikh Zaid, promising to receive the Sultan of Abu Dhabi in early winter. The Sultan also agreed to consider making a recording for the BBC about his plans to develop the sultanate after oil export commenced. However, the Sultan refused permission for the BBC to film in Oman.[48]

In August, the SAF held a demonstration of firepower on the outskirts of Salalah. The Sultan attended. Several thousand Dhofaris at the display accorded their ruler a warm reception. British observers were pleased that the Sultan appeared popular, but were quick to point out that the warmth of the Sultan's reception in Salalah was not an indication that he would be warmly received in the interior of Dhofar, where rebel activity continued.[49]

Meanwhile, the Sultan continued to reject almost every innovation that was suggested to him. The Trucial States Council had decided to change the driving system in their states from left to right and asked if the Sultan would agree to do the same in his domains. The Sultan refused. The sultanate and Britain were among the only countries where driving on the left was the rule. True, drivers from the Trucial States might become confused after crossing his border, but they would have to adjust. Sultan Said did, however, agree that when Britain changed its rule of the road he, too, would change Oman's. Meanwhile, he did not understand why coexistence between the two systems was a problem, claiming:

> When the Americans had been in Salalah driving in accordance with their tribal custom on the right hand side, he himself had changed over to the right, *inside* the town, in order to avoid colliding with them. Outside the town he had continued to drive on the left.[50]

Complaints against the Sultan persisted and the British Consul in Muscat continued to defend him. The Sultan had brought his country out of bankruptcy, and with the exception of Dhofar had maintained security and justice. The Sultan had also provided a few agricultural experimental stations, doctors, and clinics. But even the loyal Bill Carden had to admit that the Sultan should have done far more.[51]

Meanwhile, the Sultan's brother, Sayyid Fahr, remained unemployed and in his distress complained about his poverty. British officials continued their refusal to assist him.[52] Searching for succor, Fahr developed a close relationship with Bahrain's Director of Police and Public Security, Shaikh Mohammed bin Sulman. As a result, Sayyid Fahr was permitted to utilize a police car for his personal use. Later, when Shaikh Zaid visited Bahrain, Sayyid Fahr appeared at his *majlis* and asked for funds. Although it appeared that Shaikh Zaid refused to provide a sum large enough to undermine the Sultan, it was likely that Fahr received some sort of tip for his personal use.[53]

In the fall of 1967, escorted by the SAF, Briton Martin Buckmaster toured the sultanate visiting the Shariqiyah, the Jebel Akhdar, the Batinah, the Wadi Hawasinah, Ibri, and Buraimi. While in Shariqiyah, Buckmaster was impressed with the sophistication of the Harth shaikhs, who spoke and wrote good classical Arabic, listened diligently to BBC news and were prepared to discuss a variety of subjects, including the Common Market. Strictly observing Ibadhi teachings, the Harth did not drink, smoke, or permit their daughters to have dolls. Buckmaster praised the young Harth shaikhs. He also compared them with their peers on the Trucial Coast. According to Buckmaster, the latter were 'for the most part, dissolute and idle, all too often addicted to drink, at best only semi-literate, neglectful in their religious observances, and lacking in any but the most superficial interest in the welfare of their people or the affairs of the world.'[54]

Buckmaster claimed that the leader of the Harth, Shaikh Ahmad bin Muhammad Al Harthi, was more prosperous than other Omani shaikhs. His hospitality was lavish. Breakfast consisted of 43 dishes, 'an appalling gastronomic ordeal.' Shaikh Ahmad had a fleet of Land Rovers, evidence that he had received considerable financial assistance from the Sultan. Other Shaikhs had pleaded for even one Land Rover or at least a license to purchase the vehicle, but the Sultan had ignored their pleas. Shaikh Ahmad's wealth did not make him universally popular. Some critics claimed that he hoarded his wealth and showed little concern for the people under his control, the Harth, the Hajriyin, and the Wahibah.[55]

Continuing on his journey, Buckmaster visited the village of Hawiyah, where Shaikh Hamdan bin Salim grew roses, jasmine, and tiger lilies. From Hawiyah, Buckmaster traveled to the camp of Shaikh Muhammad bin Hamad of the Wahibah, where the feasts of the Harth were replaced by 'the crudest bedu fare.' There, in the sand, the camel maintained supremacy. Then Buckmaster moved on to the Jebel Akhdar. He enjoyed the hot springs of Nakhl and Rostaq. Climbing the mountain, the Englishman remarked on the friendliness of the people. He also noted that the villagers had not totally recovered from the disruption caused by the rebellion. A considerable number of the members of two tribes, the Beni Riyam and the Beni Hina, had participated in the rebellion. As a result, the Sultan had forbidden members of these tribes to leave Oman. The ban on travel excluded young men from employment in other Gulf States. Limited to their territory, they worked hard to restore the local fruit trees and vines. Farmers on the Akhdar produced grapes, peaches, figs, almonds, pomegranates, limes, walnuts, and even roses.[56]

At the conclusion of his tour, Buckmaster reported that, despite some grumbling against the Sultan, Omanis were fundamentally conservative and not at all interested in Sayyid Tariq's attempts to oust their ruler. Omanis 'want more from the Sultan, and chafe at some of the restrictions he imposed on them, but most give him credit for having restored security to a troubled land.' The country remained poor, but those Omanis permitted to work abroad were sending money home, and now that oil had started to flow there was anticipation of a better future.[57]

In November 1967, when Minister of State Goronwy Roberts toured the Gulf States to assure the rulers that Britain intended to remain in the region, Roberts told the Sultan that events in Aden might necessitate an evacuation of British military personnel to Masirah by ship. Although the British had an agreement with the Sultan to use Masirah, the agreement only covered landing by air. Roberts said that he would be grateful if the Sultan would now permit landings by sea. The Sultan agreed. Political Resident Crawford, who had accompanied Roberts to Salalah, informed the Sultan that with the agreement of the inhabitants of those islands, Britain was prepared to return the Kuria Muria Islands to him. The Sultan was pleased, and despite his aversion to newspaper reporters, even agreed that in the spring of 1968 he would permit a *New York Times* correspondent to visit the sultanate.[58]

While in Salalah, Roberts also discussed the importance of improving conditions in Dhofar and in the rest of the country. Roberts told the Sultan that he ought to consider presenting a better image to the world. The Sultan appeared uninterested, but Minister of State Roberts considered it still possible to impress the Omani ruler.[59]

Meanwhile, in London, the *Sunday Times* published an interview with Sayyid Tariq, now in Dubai. The Sultan's brother spoke passionately. He said that he would assume leadership of all Omani dissidents and claimed that it was imperative to 'get rid of the Sultan.'[60]

Britain had no wish to encourage Sayyid Tariq and continued to prod the reluctant Sultan toward development. Political Resident Sir Stewart told the Foreign Office that the Sultan had prepared a manifesto that spelled out his plans. According to Crawford, the Sultan was a man of his word; he kept his promises.[61] Finally, in January 1968, the Sultan distributed his manifesto:

> We guarantee raising the standard of living of the inhabitants of the Sultanate and increasing the income of the individual. We shall develop the country to keep pace with present-day civilization. We shall ensure every benefit and advantage for the people.[62]

From Muscat, Bill Carden reviewed the Sultan's practices, telling London that the Sultan was a fairly kindly despot. Carden was convinced that, after 30 years as ruler, Sultan Said knew his country well and would be able to balance fairly between competing claims from different sections. The Sultan was an honorable man and 'unlike many Heads of State or Ministers in the Middle East, is a man whose word, given in this manner, is his bond.'[63]

Yet, the Sultan continued to delay development. He remained unwilling to bring his people the benefits of modern education and healthcare. Nor was he prepared to listen to those who disagreed with him. As a result, while Britain defended the ruler from his enemies both at home and abroad, the sultanate remained undeveloped.

NOTES

1. Miriam Joyce, *The Sultanate of Oman: A Twentieth Century History* (Westport, CT: Praeger, 1995), pp. 27–8.
2. Ibid, pp. 56–9.
3. Letter, Phillips to Mann, Muscat, 23 June 1960, FO 371/148906, PRO.
4. Letter, Phillips to Foreign Office, Muscat, 23 March 1962, FO 371/162844, PRO.
5. The Oman and Muscat Committee, Arabian Department, London, 2 April 1962, FO 371/162844, PRO.
6. Minute, London, 16 December 1961, FO 371/162843, PRO.

7.   Letter, Phillips to Walmsley, Muscat, 24 March 1962, FO 371/162844, PRO.
8.   Letter, Luce to Walmsley, Bahrain, 30 April 1962, FO 371/162845, PRO.
9.   Ibid.
10. Telegram 177, British Embassy to Foreign Office, Kuwait, 25 March 1962, FO 371/162844, PRO.
11. Letter, Phillips to Luce, Muscat, 3 May 1962, FO 371/162845, PRO.
12. Letter, Luce to Walmsley, Bahrain, 16 May 1962, FO 371/162845, PRO.
13. Minute, Black, London, 13 June 1962, FO 371/16284, PRO.
14. Letter, Buckley to Taylor, London, 17 April 1963, T 317/197, PRO.
15. Telegram 18, Dean to Foreign Office, New York, 4 January 1962, FO 371/162850, PRO.
16. Brief for Secretary of State for War, London, 7 January 1963, FO 371/162850, PRO.
17. Joyce, *The Sultanate of Oman*, pp. 96–7.
18. Margaret Luce, *From Aden to the Gulf: Personal Diaries, 1956–1966* (Wiltshire: Michael Russell, 1987), p. 191.
19. Quoted in Letter, Carden to Luce, Muscat, 12 May 1966, FO 371/185364, PRO.
20. Muscat Annual Report for 1964, FO 371/179813, PRO.
21. Telegram 338, Mann to Foreign Office, Jedda, 18 July 1965, FO 371/179815, PRO.
22. Telegram 684, Phillips to Foreign Office, Bahrain, 18 August 1965, FO 371/179815, PRO.
23. Letter, Brown to McCarthy, Jedda, 24 July 1965, FO 371/179815, PRO, and Letter, Phillips to Arabian Department, Bahrain, 11 August 1965, FO 371/179815, PRO.
24. Letter, Gandy to Weir, Kuwait, 7 December 1965, FO 371/179815, PRO.
25. Letter, Jackson to Brenchley, Kuwait, 12 December 1965, FO 371/179815, PRO.
26. Letter, Carden to Weir, Muscat, 22 December 1965, FO 371/179815, PRO.
27. Telegram 147, Foreign Office to Cairo, London, 20 May 1966, FO 371/185364, PRO.
28. Letter, Carden to Stewart, Muscat, Note 2, 25 January 1968, FCO 8/574, PRO.
29. Letter, Carden to Luce, Muscat, 12 May 1966, FO 371/185364, PRO.
30. Memorandum, London, 21 November 1966, FO 371/185364, PRO.
31. Letter, Carden to Luce, Muscat, 11 May 1966. FO 371/185364, PRO.
32. Ibid.
33. Letter, Luce to Carden, Bahrain, 27 May 1966, FO 371/185364, PRO.
34. Letter, Carden to Balfour-Paul, Muscat, 29 September 1966, FO 371/185364, PRO.
35. Ibid.
36. Letter, Carden to Balfour-Paul, Muscat, 15 October 1966, FO 371/185531, PRO.
37. Letter, Balfour-Paul to Lamb, Bahrain, 10 October 1966, FO 371/ 185531, PRO.
38. Letter, Carden to Crawford, Muscat, 26 October 1966, FO 371/185531, PRO.
39. Letter, Lamb to Crawford, Abu Dhabi, 6 November 1966, FO 371/185531, PRO.
40. Letter, Carden to Meadows, Muscat, 14 March 1967, FCO 8/574, PRO.
41. Minute, Graham, London, 16 February 1967, FCO 8/574, PRO.
42. Talk with the Sultan, Crawford, Salalah, 10 March 1967, FCO 8/574, PRO.
43. Talk with the Sultan, Crawford, Salalah, 10 March 1967, FCO 8/574, PRO.
44. Telegram, unnumbered, Muscat to Foreign Office, 1 May 1967, FCO 8/575, PRO.

45. Memorandum, Crawford, London, 13 May 1967, FCO 8/575, PRO.
46. Letter, Roberts to Carden, Dubai, 1 July 1967, FCO 8/575, PRO.
47. Letter, Carden to Roberts, Muscat, 4 July 1967, Muscat, FCO 8/575, PRO.
48. Letter, Carden to Crawford, Muscat, 13 July 1967, FCO 8/574, PRO.
49. Letter, Pragnell to Melhuish, Muscat, 2 September 1967, FCO 8/574, PRO.
50. Letter, Balfour-Paul to Pragnell, Bahrain, 8 September 1966, FO 371/185364, PRO.
51. Letter, Carden to Moore, Muscat, 1 October 1966, FO 371/185364, PRO.
52. Letter, Clark to Pragnall, Dubai, 17 September 1967, FCO 8/575, PRO.
53. Letter, Parsons to Carden, Bahrain,19 October 1967, FCO 8/575, PRO.
54. Letter, Buckmaster to Balfour-Paul, Dubai, 25 October 1967, FCO 8/576, PRO.
55. Ibid.
56. Ibid.
57. Ibid.
58. Record of a Conversation, Salalah, 6 November 1967, FCO 8/144, PRO.
59. Minute, Stirling, London, 28 November 1967, FCO 8/144, PRO.
60. *Sunday Times*, London, 20 November 1966, FO 371/185364, PRO.
61. Letter, Crawford to Brenchley, Bahrain, 27 December 1967, FCO 8/574, PRO.
62. Summary of Booklet, Muscat, January 1968, FCO 8/574, PRO.
63. Note, Carden to Foreign Office, Muscat, 25 January 1968, FO 371/FCO 8/574, PRO.

6

1968: Year of decision

At the beginning of January 1968, Minister of State for Foreign Affairs Goronwy Roberts once more traveled to the Gulf. Rulers of the protected states were not pleased. When the government of Bahrain learned that so soon after his initial visit the British Minister of State was calling a second time, the Al Khalifa shaikhs immediately realized that his purpose was not 'to wish them a Happy New Year.'[1]

London was now prepared to change course. Motivated by the need to economize, the British government had decided to relinquish its traditional role in the Gulf region. Shortly before the dramatic news of HMG's intended withdrawal was announced in Parliament, Roberts was despatched to inform the rulers of this decision. After learning that, in 1971, Britain would leave their domain, rulers of the Gulf States expressed shock. Qatar's ruler, Shaikh Ahmed Al Thani, protested that London's decision to announce withdrawal was a mistake; that Britain had responsibilities in the region and ought not to relinquish them because of 'pressure from people of no consequence in the United Kingdom.' Roberts explained that Britain's financial position had worsened, that the British 'had to make sacrifices at home and abroad.' He said that the rulers ought now to join forces to create a new system to ensure their security.[2]

Shaikh Ahmed Al Khalifa remained angry. Britain had a treaty with his shaikhdom. Announcing withdrawal prior to consultation was dishonorable. The British were ignoring their commitments. Withdrawal would assist the Soviets and Arab revolutionary governments. Shaikh Ahmed also feared that the departure of British troops would end prosperity in his region: that chaos would follow.[3]

Kuwait's amir, Shaikh Sabah Al Sabah, was stunned by the announcement.[4] He was especially concerned about Bahrain, which had half the total Arab population of the nine states and was in danger of being seized by the Shah, 'to whom the Western powers paid such court as an asset in the context of East–West confrontation.'[5] Since Shaikh Sabah had already planned an official visit to Iran, he now decided that one of the priorities of his visit would be to convince the Shah to recognize Bahrain as part of the Arab nation.[6]

On 8 January, Roberts met in Bahrain with members of the Al Khalifa family, Shaikh Isa, Shaikh Khalifa, and Shaikh Mohammed. Explaining that Britain had serious financial problems, that the cost of maintaining commitments all over the world was too high for one small country, Roberts announced that HMG had decided to withdraw from both the Far East and the Gulf by 31 March 1971. During the interim period, Britain would continue to protect the Gulf States, but in order to safeguard their future the states would have to settle their previous differences, and come together to prepare for the post-British era.[7]

Bahraini shaikhs expressed fear that Britain's declaration would severely damage Bahrain's economy. Shaikh Isa quickly arranged for a two-day visit to Saudi Arabia to consult King Faisal.[8] At the same time, still hoping to convince Britain to stay, he offered to waive the £350,000 annual payment charged to HMG for military facilities.[9]

The Al Khalifa family considered the British announcement a betrayal, 'an unvarnished *volte face.*' In November 1967, the British government had reiterated its commitment to the region. Now, after 150 years, without warning or 'genuine consultation', the British planned to leave. Bahrain's rulers doubted that the various small states could achieve unity. At the same time, they were concerned about what Iran would do after the British departure and were also worried about the possibility that, anticipating an Iranian or Nasserite takeover of Bahrain, Saudi Arabia might strike first. Deputy ruler Shaikh Khalifa Al Khalifa suggested that the British were leaving Bahrain to be 'kicked like a football between the players in the Gulf game.' Considering their alternatives, on 12 January the Bahraini leadership appeared to view statehood and a defense treaty with Saudi Arabia as the 'most practical of a bad lot of alternatives.'[10]

Dubai's ruler, Shaikh Rashid Al Maktum, warned British officials that the Gulf States might transfer their sterling balances to whatever power assumed the role of their major protector.[11] Ruler of Abu Dhabi Shaikh Zaid Al Nuhayyan said that he had always understood that Britain's presence in the region was temporary, but he considered it wrong for the British to leave before they had assisted in the construction of a system that would unite the rulers.[12] Meeting alone with Political Agent Archie Lamb, Shaikh Zaid said that earlier, senior merchants from Dubai, Sharjah and Abu Dhabi had called on him and suggested that he assume the position of leader in Trucial Oman. These merchants claimed that, of all the rulers, 'he was the only one whose heart was with the people.' Shaikh Zaid discussed his rival, Shaikh Rashid, whom he claimed wished to retain all power for himself. Instead of turning to him, his neighbor and fellow Bani Yas, Shaikh Rashid, had asked Saudi Arabia for a loan. According to Shaikh Zaid, the ruler of Dubai was afraid that he, Zaid Al Nuhayyan, would use his wealth to take over Dubai, but that was not his plan: 'he wanted to live in peace, friendship and cooperation with Shaikh Rashid.'[13]

Clearly, Shaikh Zaid considered himself to be the most suitable candidate to lead the Gulf shaikhdoms. In addition to criticizing Shaikh Rashid, he found shortcomings in the ruler of Ras Al Khaimah, whom he claimed was interested only in his own grandeur, and the ruler of Sharjah, whom he labeled insecure. As for the other three rulers, of Ajman, Umm Al Qawain, and Fujairah, they 'were not worth talking about.'[14] In 1968, Ajman's ruler, Shaikh Rashid bin Hamid Al Nuaimi, who depended on funding from stamps that he issued, which were popular with philatelists, continued to live in a baked clay castle without electricity. Ruler of Umm Al Qawain, Shaikh Ahmed bin Rashid Al Mu'alla, was worse off, depending only on limited trade in fish and tobacco.[15]

Among Gulf rulers, Sultan Said bin Taimour alone appeared unconcerned about Britain's impending departure. He maintained that HMG had no obligation to defend the sultanate and since none of his agreements with Britain were affected, he had no reason to object to the proposed British withdrawal. According to the Sultan, for 30 years he had been dealing with Omani tribes, and as long as his rule was strong but kindly he would maintain the confidence of his people. The task of a ruler was clear. 'It was always to do that which in his judgement would be best for his people.' But British officials were less sanguine about the future of the sultanate. It appeared that the Sultan had an 'almost pathological inability' to delegate responsibility. Now 58 years old, Sultan Said selected advisers who were even older. His own son, Sayyid Qaboos, remained completely cut off from affairs of state, 'rather a pathetic figure;' his father continued to refuse to name a successor.[16]

At the same time that the protected states were informed of Britain's decision to leave the Gulf, so too was the Shah of Iran informed. 'He raised no objection and began immediately to plan to take over the hegemony of the Gulf area.' Later, however, after the Iraqi Baath party took power in July 1968, it appeared likely that, in the Gulf, Iran would have to compete with Iraq.[17]

The seven Trucial State rulers met on 13 January in Umm Al Qawain, where many shaikhs appeared to be 'in a state of panic.'[18] Four days later, on 17 January, Prime Minister Harold Wilson publicly announced plans to withdraw the British military from both the Far East and the Gulf. After the Prime Minister's announcement, one irate Conservative MP claimed that Britain's oil operations would be in jeopardy 'the very moment our troops leave the Persian Gulf.' He warned that the protected states would be unable to maintain their independence, that the Soviets might gain control. The agitated MP said that it was 'quite monstrous' for such a decision to be announced prior to discussion in the House of Commons.[19]

On 20 January, Kuwait's National Assembly discussed the British decision to withdraw from the region. Some deputies urged that after the British left no foreign power be permitted to interfere in Gulf affairs. But other deputies suggested that the scenario for their future had already been decided for them, that 'American and Eshkol' would replace Britain. Kuwait's Prime Minister counseled that the deputies resist believing every rumor that circulated.[20]

On behalf of the four major rulers, Dubai's, Shaikh Rashid was authorized to suggest that HMG allow the Gulf States to assume the cost of maintaining a British military presence. According to Shaikh Rashid, if the British accepted the offer to defend the Gulf after 1971, their troops would not be mercenaries, but allies engaged in the maintenance of peace and stability. Political Resident Crawford was pleased that the rulers were willing to assume the financial burden of keeping the British in the Gulf. He asked the Foreign Office for guidance.[21] Meanwhile, Foreign Office officials in the Gulf speculated about whether or not Kuwait was included among the states willing to contribute funds to keep the British in place.[22]

Defense Secretary Denis Healey was opposed to accepting Arab aid. During a BBC television interview on 22 January, he said that it was a grave mistake to permit British troops to become mercenaries. 'I don't very much like the idea of being a sort of white slaver for Arab sheikhs.' Admitting that the Gulf remained an area of vital importance, Healey said that in the period prior to withdrawal, Britain had to work hard to create stability. According to the Defense Minister:

> We can not by ourselves guarantee peace and stability all over the world without going bankrupt or borrowing very large sums of money from

other people. Now in the field of defence and foreign policy, and let me tell you my job as Defence Secretary is not to decide our commitments but to make certain that if we cut our capability we cut our commitments.[23]

After Healey's interview, Kuwait's Minister of Guidance and Information expressed agreement with the Defense Secretary's unwillingness to accept contributions for the British military, but objected to how Healey stated his views. The Defense Secretary authorized a statement expressing regret for some of his phrases.[24] Then the Foreign Office instructed its officials in the Gulf to thank the rulers for their offer of financial assistance, but given British commitments in Europe, even with financial aid, it would be impossible for HMG to provide the logistic backing that a military presence in the Gulf required.[25]

Worried about the future security of his state, Amir Sabah considered where he would turn for military assistance after the British departure. In the middle of January it appeared that Kuwait was considering a defense arrangement with both Iran and Saudi Arabia, but decided that inclusion of Iraq was essential. If Iraq were not a member, Cairo would brand the group reactionary, and Kuwait was unwilling to risk losing Egyptian support.[26]

Meanwhile, Qatar sought American support. At the end of February, a representative of Shaikh Khalifa Al Thani, William Kazzan, called at the American Embassy in Beirut. According to Kazzan, Qatar was concerned by the sudden British decision to leave the region before the end of 1971. His confidence in Britain shaken, Qatar's deputy ruler, Shaikh Khalifa Al Thani, wanted the void created by that decision filled. In order to resist pressure from those he considered 'too Arab', he wanted moral support from the great powers. When the British departed he wished to hire American and other non-Arab advisers.[27] Kazzan emphasized that Qatar wanted to obtain support for its independence. The Qataris were not convinced that a federation would resolve the problems posed by British withdrawal and were concerned that, without the support of a great power, they would be unable to resist leftist Arab elements. Hence, deputy ruler Shaikh Khalifa Al Thani wished to visit the United States and discuss his views with the State Department.[28]

American officials in Beirut explained to Kazzan that the correct channel for American contact with the Gulf States, that as yet retained their special treaty relations with Britain, was through the Consul

General in Dhahran.[29] American Secretary of State Dean Rusk instructed the American Embassy in Lebanon that if Kazzan again proposed that the Qatari deputy ruler visit the United States, American officials respond that Shaikh Khalifa was welcome to visit 'in purely private capacity,' but that he was unlikely to find a private visit satisfactory.

> Until emerging situation in Gulf evolves further permitting clearer determination what USG may be in position to do in this area, discussions of the type contemplated by Kazzan with local Rulers would be counterproductive.[30]

Then, in March, the British in Doha were concerned about an incident that tarnished the reputation of the Al Thani family. As a result of a minor traffic accident, one of Shaikh Ahmed's nephews, Abdul Rahman bin Mohammad bin Ali, a member of what the Political Agent called 'the Abdul-Rahman gang', approached a home belonging to members of the Beni Ahmed. Shots were fired and one of the Beni Ahmed was killed. The ruler's nephew, Abdul Rahman, drove to the Doha Police Station and there threatened the police until the quick arrival of the British Commandant averted further trouble. After leaving the police station, the angry Abdul Rahman and his men arrived at the hospital brandishing machine guns. Abdul Rahman was arrested and taken to prison.[31] Following weeks of discussion, the ruler's nephew was executed in his cell. Political Agent Ranald Boyle was convinced that the ruler acted wisely. According to the Political Agent:

> I am fairly certain that if a death sentence had not been carried out, the Al Thani family would ultimately have been doomed. As it is, Sheikh Ahmed's strong line and considerable resolution in the face of the pleas and arguments of his father, brothers and their families for Abdul Rahman's life have given him increased stature; if he can keep it up, a 'new' Ahmed may have emerged as head of a rapidly developing state.[32]

Boyle hoped that that members of the ruling family would now be prohibited from carrying guns in Doha and that the wild behavior of young family members would be curbed. On 21 March, Shaikh Ahmed met with family members at Rayyan Palace, where he delivered a stern lecture.[33]

Meanwhile, the rulers of the seven Trucial States, together with the rulers of Qatar and Bahrain, continued deliberations. They decided to attempt a union of nine. Soon after London had announced Britain's intended withdrawal, Shaikhs Zaid Al Nuhayyan and Rashid Al Maktum had encouraged discussion among the nine shaikhdoms. Wealthy Shaikh Zaid continued efforts to bring the states together under his leadership; Shaikh Rashid, however, still did not wish to be dominated by Shaikh Zaid. Nevertheless, on 16 February, the two shaikhs met. Shaikh Zaid agreed to provide his neighbor with a large interest-free loan. He also agreed to transfer a strip of seabed 10 kilometres wide to Dubai. As a result, the two rulers consented to a union of Abu Dhabi and Dubai. Together they issued an invitation to the other Trucial States to join them in a union under one flag.[34] The British hoped that the agreement between Shaikh Zaid and Shaikh Rashid would be sufficiently successful to encourage the other states.

Meanwhile, rebel activity persisted in Dhofar. The Sultan's opponents continued to strike at his authority. Concerned with the security of Petroleum Development Oman, Political Resident Crawford advised that HMG work to ensure the continuation of the Al Bu Said dynasty. Sir Stewart claimed that loss of Dhofar would weaken the authority of 'whoever is Sultan.'[35] Sultan Said showed every indication that he wished to remain in control. Preparing for the departure of the British, the Sultan authorized the purchase of additional airplanes for his military. He also authorized an increase in pay for his armed forces and invited a British mission to advise him on establishment of an effective navy. The ruler also took steps to establish contacts with other states. As a result, Iranian, French, and Japanese diplomats visited Muscat. By April, the rebels in Dhofar were continuing to yield ground. Nevertheless, the Sultan still refused to allow journalists into his country.[36]

Although the Sultan appeared self-confident, the British remained concerned about the future of the sultanate. In January, Consul General Bill Carden had again considered the possibility that a Dhofari rebel might assassinate the Sultan. Carden now suggested that if the Sultan were killed, that Sayyid Tariq quickly return to Oman and attempt to establish a more liberal government with Sayyid Qaboos as Sultan. The Consul General speculated that the uncle and nephew would endeavor to make peace with the imamate, and resolve disputes with Saudi Arabia.[37]

Sir Stewart agreed that it was in Britain's interest to preserve the Al Bu Said dynasty. He suggested that in the event of Sultan Said's death, it would not be sufficient for only Sayyid Tariq to return to Muscat: that Sayyid Fahr, too, ought to return home. According to the Political Resident, the family should select Sultan Said's successor and it would be unwise for Britain to interfere in that decision. He considered Sayyid Qaboos supported by Sayyid Tariq to be 'the best bet.' However, Sir Stewart told London that he remained convinced that, for the years ahead, 'whatever his shortcomings', Sultan Said ought to remain in place. Yes, Sayyid Tariq was more liberal and more flexible than his brother the Sultan, but at the same time, he was 'nothing like so strong a personality.'[38]

In April, Abu Dhabi's ruler, Shaikh Zaid Al Nuhayyan, finally visited the Sultan in Salalah. The visit was successful. Both rulers agreed to military cooperation. They planned to standardize radio equipment to link their armies and to communicate directly with each other. The Sultan also suggested that Oman and Abu Dhabi link their currencies. In so far as concerned progress in the sultanate, Shaikh Zaid told the Political Resident that development was moving too slowly, that people would lose patience.[39] This meeting between the rulers of Oman and Abu Dhabi led to speculation in Bahrain that perhaps the Sultan was interested in joining the United Arab Emirates (UAE). Bahrainis did not support Omani membership because 'they feel that the Sultan has about 600 years of leeway to make up before he could be acceptable even in present day Gulf terms.'[40]

Shaikh Zaid Al Nuhayyan continued to work toward union. The first conference of the nine rulers had been held in Dubai between 25 and 27 February. On the second day of the meeting a crisis developed when Shaikh Zaid insisted that the seven other shaikhdoms accede to the earlier Dubai/Abu Dhabi union. Qatar and Bahrain refused. With British assistance a compromise was reached. Only the preamble of the agreement to establish a nine-member UAE mentioned the earlier union of Dubai and Abu Dhabi. After the meeting the rulers issued a joint communiqué, which referred to 'an atmosphere of brotherhood, affection and understanding.'[41] One British official wrote:

> It is very much a lawyer's attempt at constitution-making, signed in haste and under pressure and with a desire to 'paper over the cracks.' Its future must depend not so much on the merits or otherwise of its *prima facie* harmless provisions as on the real stake which the participants see themselves as having in it.[42]

Britain considered the agreement satisfactory. According to Whitehall, the rulers might be surprised to learn that they had created an entity 'not dissimilar to the Arab League.'[43] While favoring a Gulf union that resembled the Arab League, London continued to object to the opening of an Arab League office in the Gulf and hoped to mobilize Saudi Arabia and Kuwait to oppose such an office. However, the British Embassy in Kuwait expressed doubt that it would be possible for Kuwait to stand up to League pressure.[44] ·

After the Dubai meeting of the nine rulers, Shaikh Zaid told Political Agent Archie Lamb that he was dissatisfied with the agreement he had signed. According to Shaikh Zaid, he wished to maintain the union of Abu Dhabi and Dubai and wanted the other Trucial States to join. Shaikh Zaid had received encouragement from Kuwaiti official Badral Khalid, who advised that he 'go all out for the unity of Trucial Oman', and that such a unit would be in a position to cooperate effectively with Bahrain and Qatar. Shaikh Zaid Al Nuhayyan insisted that he wanted good relations with all of his neighbors, but that Qatar was not willing to cooperate. 'Whatever he [Zaid] proposed, Ahmed opposed.' Shaikh Zaid claimed that he was disappointed with HMG and did not approve of the British policy of non-interference in the negotiations among the Gulf States.[45]

Meanwhile, the ruler of Fujairah expressed objection to Qatar's suggestion that in future meetings the five small Trucial States should have one vote among them and be represented by one ruler.[46] However, Qatar's deputy ruler Shaikh Khalifa Al Thani was pleased with the meeting's results. He was optimistic about the future. Practical details had not been worked out, but had been left for the next meeting. Shaikh Khalifa Al Thani considered the agreement between the nine states 'a tender plant,' which the British would join in tending. However, adviser to the Qatari government Dr Hassan Kamal continued to worry. He expressed regret that despite his pleas to omit the term, the agreement included the words 'Arabia Gulf,' a phrase that would certainly provoke Iran.[47]

Now, Shaikh Zaid Al Nuhayyan insisted that the army command and Ministry of Foreign Affairs be located in Abu Dhabi. He also emphasized the need to keep Qatar inside the UAE. Shaikh Zaid claimed that Qatari membership would deter future Saudi aggression.[48] But it appeared to some Gulf shaikhs that Abu Dhabi's ruler intended to dominate the other six Trucial States. Dubai's ruler Shaikh Rashid was annoyed and now complained that Shaikh Zaid drew workers away from Dubai and Ras Al Khaimah, 'seducing the bedu to seek easy money and avoid work.'[49]

Shaikh Rashid stated that if Shaikh Zaid truly wanted to help development in the Trucial States, he ought to work through the Rulers' Council and the Development Office. Shaikh Rashid assured the Political Resident that if the ruler of Abu Dhabi agreed to operate through the Council and Development Office, that Dubai would continue to strive for the unity of the seven Trucial States within a larger union that included Qatar and Bahrain.[50] Meanwhile, Shaikh Zaid pressed on, requesting a meeting of delegates from all the states to form a committee to draft a constitution.[51]

Bahrain signed the agreement to enter the union, but at the same time Shaikh Isa appeared interested in moving alone toward an independent Bahrain with full membership of the United Nations. According to Political Resident Sir Stewart Crawford:

> I imagine that it will be possible for the Ruler if he is careful to ride both horses for some time without having to come off either, especially if we are right in thinking that it would not be practical politics to try to get Bahrain (or the Union if this proves the better long-distance runner) into the United Nations before 1971.[52]

The Shah of Iran had reacted negatively to the announcement of the union. On 1 April, the Iranian government had issued a statement denouncing the union:

> British Government cannot bequeath to others territories that it has...severed from Iran by force and treachery. The Imperial Iranian Government reserves all its rights in the Persian Gulf...and will under no circumstances tolerate this historical injustice and imposition.[53]

According to the Shah, all of Bahrain, the island of Abu Musa, which was ruled by Sharjah, and the two Tunb Islands ruled by Ras Al Khaimah, belonged to Iran. The Shah asserted that the creation of the UAE prejudiced his claim to that territory.[54]

Tehran was especially hostile to Bahrain's membership. Hence, Shaikhs Rashid and Ahmed wished to avoid further provoking the Shah. In April, Shaikh Isa sent out invitations for the next meeting of rulers, which was scheduled for 19 May in Bahrain. Although Bahrain had earlier been chosen as the location for the meeting of the nine, the rulers of Dubai and Qatar requested that the site be changed. Shaikh Isa acquiesced.[55] At this juncture, union did not appear promising. Although Shaikh Zaid had earlier agreed to provide considerable additional funds for development, he had not yet done so.[56]

Finally, however, Shaikh Zaid Al Nuhayyan began to offer other rulers financial assistance, but in return asked for their political support. On 25 May the rulers met in Abu Dhabi. Here the four northern rulers of Sharjah, Ajman, Umm al Qawain, and Fujairah gave their full support to their rich uncle in Abu Dhabi.[57] Shaikh Zaid's success distressed the rulers of Dubai and Qatar. Bahrain's Shaikh Isa, however, distrusted Qatar and as a result was drawn to Abu Dhabi. Qatar and Dubai wanted the first order of business to be selection of a capital and a president. Supported by Qatar, Shaikh Rashid Al Maktum insisted that the capital must be Dubai. Shaikh Isa wanted Bahrain but realized that Iranian opposition to the entire enterprise ruled out his territory and so selected not Dubai but Abu Dhabi. Shaikh Zaid wholeheartedly agreed.[58]

Sir Stewart Crawford was not optimistic that the rulers could overcome their differences. He claimed:

> The divisions between the two camps have become sharper, the Rulers are not adept at finding compromises, and the long-standing rivalries between some of them make them believe the worst of each other.[59]

Yet, the Political Resident did not relinquish hope for union. In May, Qatar's ruler Shaikh Ahmed Al Thani arrived in Kuwait for a state visit. According to American officials in Kuwait, the visit was 'a symbolic hatchet burying' between the Al Sabahs and the Al Thani families, who had often been at odds. After Shaikh Ahmed's departure, the Kuwaiti Foreign Ministry issued a statement saying that the Amir had assured Shaikh Ahmed that Kuwait welcomed the establishment of a United Arab Emirates, which included Qatar.[60] But while publicly expressing support for the union of nine, Kuwaiti Foreign Ministry officials privately told American diplomats that they doubted that the union would be accomplished.[61]

Cairo and Baghdad also expressed support for merger of the small states. Saudi Arabia too continued to favor unity. Sir Stewart discussed the problems dividing members of the proposed union with Qatar's deputy ruler Shaikh Khalifa Al Thani. The Qatari shaikh was concerned that the period until Britain's 1971 withdrawal was too brief; that there was not enough time for the Gulf States to prepare. After explaining that HMG had no proposals to put forward to achieve agreement, Sir Stewart made a personal suggestion. Since agreement on where to establish the capital had not been reached, why not build a new town, a town that bordered two of the shaikhdoms? The Political Resident also suggested that one of the rulers be appointed interim President.[62]

Following months of uncertainty, on 27 June Shaikh Rashid bin Said Al Maktum visited the House of Commons. Minister of State for Foreign Affairs Goronwy Roberts asked Dubai's ruler for his assessment of prospects for establishment of the UAE. Shaikh Rashid was not optimistic. He claimed that his neighbor, Shaikh Zaid, opposed a union of all nine states. According to Shaikh Rashid, the ruler of Abu Dhabi was building a personal defense force which could in future threaten Dubai. As a result, he was considering establishing a force of his own. Roberts reminded Shaikh Rashid that Abu Dhabi had a long frontier to guard and therefore might very well consider Shaikh Zaid's force essential. Roberts assured Shaikh Rashid that sufficient time remained for the Gulf States to prepare to assume responsibility for security. He hoped that, rather than build independent forces, the rulers would cooperate and together support the Trucial Oman Scouts, which could become their joint force.[63]

On 23 June, the Kuwaiti Foreign Minister Shaikh Sabah had visited Bahrain, his first stop on a tour of the Gulf. Kuwait wished to help move formation of the UAE forward. The Foreign Minister had several proposals, including postponement of the selection of a site for a capital. He also advised that, rather than immediately select a president, the rulers elect a different chairman for each meeting of their Supreme Council. Shaikh Sabah also spoke to Hassan Kamal and told him to remember local conditions, 'to compromise in favour of results and not to stand pat on complicated legal formulae.' Speaking to British officials, Shaikh Sabah asked that HMG continue efforts to promote the UAE. Warning of possible Soviet activity, he stressed that failure of the UAE would not be beneficial for the states of the region or for Britain. As for Iran, the Kuwaiti expressed confidence that as soon as the UAE was a reality the Shah would extend recognition.[64] British officials, too, continued to consider establishment of the UAE 'the best hope of least disturbance on our departure.'[65]

In Bahrain, a majority of the members of the ruling family and a large number of established merchants remained doubtful. Bahrainis considered themselves to be far more advanced than the inhabitants of the other shaikhdoms. Nevertheless, younger Bahrainis remained enthusiastic about the concept of Arab unity and therefore favored Bahrain's membership. At the same time, all Bahrainis continued to worry about Iranian intentions, and to many it appeared that union might provide a measure of security that would be denied Bahrain as an independent mini-state.[66]

Clinging to the claim that Bahrain belonged to Iran, the Shah's government continued adamantly to oppose such a union and was offended that London was working to achieve it. British officials tried to assure Iran that London favored improved relations between the Persian and Arab sides of the Gulf. In July, the British informed Tehran that progress toward the formation of a Union of Arab shaikhdoms was slow and that numerous problems remained to be resolved.[67] During dinner at the Iranian Embassy in London, British officials suggested that separate statehood for Bahrain might be less advantageous to Iran than Bahrain's inclusion in a union of Gulf States. As an independent state Bahrain would be admitted to the United Nations, which 'would pose the question of the Iranian claim much more starkly than if Bahrain were absorbed in membership of a Union.' Iran's ambassador said that Tehran wished to have good relations with the Gulf States, but if Bahrain became a member of the union, then Iran's claim against one state would lead to confrontation with all eight other states. Iran wanted the British to caution the nine rulers to consider seriously the Iranian view. Sir Denis Allen assured Iran's ambassador that Britain continued to encourage improved relations between the Iranian and Arab sides of the Gulf: that HMG considered such cooperation 'the key to future stability and good order.'[68]

Despite the myriad of difficulties, Political Resident Sir Stewart urged the Foreign Office to do nothing that the rulers might interpret as an indication that London was considering the possibility of a union of less than nine: one that would exclude Bahrain. Sir Stewart feared that if Shaikh Isa stood alone, the Shah might find it easier to take Bahrain. The Political Resident emphasized that exclusion would not be in Bahrain's interest.[69]

But the nine rulers did not appear able to put aside their differences. Qatar's Shaikh Ahmed accused Bahrain and Abu Dhabi of commissioning articles in a variety of Middle Eastern publications that tarnished the reputation of Qatar and Dubai. Shaikh Ahmed Al Thani complained to the Political Agent that Shaikh Zaid 'did not know God,' that he had relations with women imported from Pakistan and Lebanon into Abu Dhabi.[70]

The rulers of the seven Trucial States, joined by the rulers of Bahrain and Qatar, met in Abu Dhabi on 6 July. Prior to the meeting, Kuwait's Foreign Minister had toured the Gulf and coaxed the rulers to compromise over procedural issues. The rulers decided that both the chairman of the Supreme Council of Rulers and the location of their meetings would rotate. They appointed committees to study the questions of currency, a postal service, a flag, and national anthem. They also decided soon to appoint a lawyer to draft a constitution. The four largest states agreed together to pay all of the union's running expenses and they deferred choosing a capital. Iran was not pleased. Claiming 'imperialists' were behind the proposed union, on 8

July the Shah's government publicly announced its opposition to Bahrain's inclusion in the UAE.[71]

Differences among shaikhs continued. During the summer, Muscat began to receive oil royalties and the British noted that Kuwait appeared to show a new interest in the sultanate. However, it was unlikely that the Sultan would wish contact with Kuwait while the Al Sabahs allowed the Imam to have an office in their state and treated the Imam's representative as a member of the Diplomatic Corps. The British Ambassador suggested that if the Kuwaitis wanted to approach the Sultan they discuss the matter with Shaikh Zaid, who had recently visited with the Omani ruler.[72]

In the summer of 1968, the Dhofaris continued to encourage rebellion, but the number of troublemakers was small, between 100 and 200. According to Bill Carden in Muscat:

> The consolidation of the Sultan's position particularly in Oman would, I should have thought, have been in the Kuwaitis' own best interest. The weaker his position the greater will be the temptation to the Saudis to grab Buraimi and to the Iranians to grab the southern side of the Gulf of Hormuz: and presumably one thing which Kuwait can do without is the start of a practice whereby large powers in the Gulf grab territory from smaller neighbors.[73]

Amir Sabah agreed that the Imam was not going to achieve victory and there was no reason to continue supporting him. At the same time, Kuwait's ruler considered the Sultan 'an absolutely dreadful man.' According to the Amir, he still did not believe that the ruler of Oman would spend his oil revenue to benefit his people and would not believe it until he had reliable evidence of development in the sultanate. Meanwhile, proprietor of a Kuwaiti newspaper, Abdul Aziz Masa'id, wished to obtain a visa to visit Oman, the only Gulf State that demanded visas from its neighbors. When informed that it was unlikely that the Sultan would admit a journalist, Masa'id suggested that Kuwait ought to expel all supporters of the Imam and abolish the necessity of visas for travel between Kuwait and Muscat.[74]

The ruler of Abu Dhabi, too, continued to express concern about conditions in Oman. Through tribal channels reports had reached Shaikh Zaid that the Sultan's subjects were unhappy. The Sultan now had the benefit of oil and still did nothing to improve conditions. Sultan Said continued to remain a recluse, who had little contact with his people. At the same time, Sayyid Qaboos continued to be a virtual prisoner, cut off from contact with the public. HMG was confident, however, that the Sultan's Armed Forces were capable of securing the ruler's territory; that there was no longer any serious danger from the rebels. Hence, the British expressed the conviction that after their departure in 1971 the Sultan would maintain control.[75]

In September 1968, the first meeting of the Federal Provincial Council took place in Doha. Defense issues now appeared to be a major stumbling block to unity and Qatar and Abu Dhabi had yet to resolve their frontier dispute. The Council achieved little.[76] Nevertheless, ruler of Bahrain Shaikh Isa considered the meeting successful. Bahrain's interest in the proposed union of nine continued. Britain persisted in coaxing the shaikhdoms toward unity, cajoling Shaikh Rashid and Shaikh Zaid to take constructive roles. The British Resident in Bahrain was satisfied that the small states were exchanging ideas. Given the legacy of internecine feuds among the shaikhs of the region, it would be unrealistic to expect to accomplish unity quickly. But head of the Foreign Office's Arabian Department, Michael Weir, was concerned about Shaikh Rashid's threats to opt out of the UAE if Shaikh Zaid did not honor the boundary agreement of February. British officials were also worried about the Dubai ruler's continuing desire to establish his own defense force. According to one official: 'If anything, the nigger in the woodpile at the moment is the Ruler of Dubai.'[77]

Shaikh Rashid protested that Abu Dhabi was building its own military force. Hence, there was no reason for him not to do the same. Rashid was concerned that Britain was encouraging Shaikh Zaid to assume the role of ultimate ruler of the UAE. All Shaikh Rashid wanted was a token force of 500 men because he was doubtful that the UAE would be able to provide the security he needed.[78]

Relations with their larger neighbors continued to be among the pressing concerns of the small shaikhdoms. In October 1968, Qatar's deputy ruler Shaikh Khalifa Al Thani visited King Faisal in Riyadh and reported that the King encouraged establishment of the UAE, but the Shah had no intention of relinquishing his claim to Bahrain, where approximately ten thousand Iranians were employed. In addition, the Shah announced that he would not recognize the UAE if Bahrain was among its members. Qatar's Shaikh Khalifa considered Iran to be the strongest power in the region and claimed that Iran alone 'would call the tune.' In addition, Shaikh Khalifa was distressed by what he claimed was Kuwait's 'patronizing attitude' toward the smaller Gulf States.[79] Nevertheless, on 29 October, in an address to the Kuwaiti National Assembly, the Amir appeared optimistic that the UAE would overcome its initial difficulties and thrive.[80] But, of course, Iran was far more patronizing than Kuwait. Following a private conversation with the Shah, the American Ambassador in Tehran reported to Washington that the Iranian ruler respected King Faisal but

> has a rather low regard for other Arabs in general. He stressed that he intends to do his best to collaborate with the trans-Gulf Arabs but they must realize that undermining the Shah's prestige and honor (he probably had the Bahrain question in mind) can only cause harm to themselves.[81]

After attending the November meeting of the UAE Provisional Council in Sharjah, Shaikh Khalifa Al Thani returned to Doha dejected. Although he admitted that some progress had been made with the establishment of various committees, he was not satisfied. He claimed that Bahrain and Abu Dhabi were slowing down the process. The issues of a single flag and a single passport had been referred back to the Supreme Council. Shaikh Khalifa was convinced that neither Bahrain nor Abu Dhabi wanted the union of nine to move forward. He suggested that the only way to overcome such resistance was for Britain to declare that HMG would in future refuse to negotiate any sort of agreement with single states, but would negotiate only with the UAE. Moreover, Shaikh Khalifa insisted that London quickly negotiate a defense agreement with the UAE, which 'would completely save the situation.'[82]

In December 1968, Foreign Office official Donal McCarthy visited Doha. Shaikh Ahmed Al Thani urged the British official to convince his government to stall arms sales to Abu Dhabi until British military experts visited the area and recommended plans for future defense. Deputy ruler Shaikh Khalifa Al Thani once more expressed the view that the union of nine shaikhdoms would survive only with British assistance, now and in the future. McCarthy insisted that Britain favored the union of nine shaikhdoms but was unwilling to make future defense commitments in the Gulf. He also emphasized that the progress of the union depended not on HMG but on the Gulf rulers themselves. 'They alone could drive the Union forward.'[83]

Meanwhile, Amir Sabah visited Washington, and on 11 December was received by President Lyndon B. Johnson. Responding to the Kuwaiti ruler's request for information about American plans in the Gulf, Assistant Secretary for Near-Eastern and South Asian Affairs Parker T. Hart said that the United States would continue to be concerned with the integrity of the Gulf States. At the same time:

We had no plans take unique place UK once held. British position developed under circumstances not existing today. People of Gulf themselves will determine future area.[84]

Hence, 1968 ended without a clear vision of what would emerge in the Gulf after the British departed. Conflicting interests continued to stand in the way of cooperation. But all of the rulers that had so relied on Britain clearly understood that to ensure the future of their shaikhly regimes they would have to proceed with efforts to organize a system that would promote the stability of the region.

NOTES

1. Ian Richard Netton (ed.) *Arabia and the Gulf: From Traditional Society to Modern States* (Totowa, NJ: Barnes & Noble, 1986), p. 183.
2. Record of a Conversation, Dubai, 11 January 1968, FCO 8/47, PRO.
3. Telegram 34, Bahrain to Foreign Office, 10 January 1968, FCO 8/47, PRO.
4. Summary Record of a Conversation, 8 January 1968, FCO 8/48, PRO.
5. Glen Balfour-Paul, *The End of Empire in the Middle East* (Cambridge: Cambridge University Press, 1991), p. 124.
6. Summary Record of a Conversation, 8 January 1968, FCO 8/48, PRO.
7. Note of a Meeting, Bahrain, 8 January 1968, FCO 8/47, PRO.
8. Minute, Arabian Department, London, 10 January 1968, FCO 8/48, PRO.
9. Telegram 37, Crawford to Foreign Office, Bahrain, 10 January 1968, FCO 8/47, PRO.
10. Letter, Parsons to Weir, Bahrain, 13 January 1968, FCO 8/48, PRO.
11. Telegram 25, Roberts to Foreign Office, Dubai, 11 January 1968, FCO 8/47, PRO.
12. Record of a Meeting, Abu Dhabi, 9 January 1968, FCO 8/47, PRO.
13. Letter, Lamb to Crawford, Abu Dhabi, 11 January 1968, FCO 8/48, PRO.
14. Ibid.
15. The *Observer*, 14 July 1968, p.8.
16. Minute, 14 February 1968, FCO 8/576, PRO.
17. Frank Brenchley, *Britain and the Middle East: An Economic History 1945–87* (London: Lester Crook, 1989), p. 170.
18. Letter, Roberts to Balfour-Paul, Dubai, 13 January 1968, FCO 8/48, PRO.
19. Hansard, Parliamentary Debates, House of Commons, 17 January 1968, pp. 1849–51.
20. Letter, Graham to Stirling, Kuwait, 21 January 1968, FCO 8/48, PRO. 'Eshkol' refers to the Prime Minister of Israel, Levi Eshkol.
21. Telegram 94, Crawford to Foreign Office, Bahrain, 24 January 1968, FCO 8/48, PRO.
22. Telegram 23, Arthur to Foreign Office, Kuwait, 14 January 1968, FCO 8/47, PRO.
23. Guidance 23, Foreign Office to Commonwealth Office, London, 23 January 1968, FCO 8/48, PRO.
24. Telegram 44, Arthur to Foreign Office, Kuwait, 25 January 1968, FCO 8/48, PRO.
25. Telegram 157, Foreign Office to Bahrain, 29 January 1968, FCO 8/48, PRO.

26. Telegram 31, Arthur to Foreign Office, Kuwait, 18 January 1968, FCO 8/47, PRO.
27. Memorandum of a Conversation, Beirut, 29 February 1968, A-775, NA.
28. Telegram 775, Porter to State Department, Beirut, 1 March 1968, Pol. 19, Qatar, NA.
29. Telegram 63, State Department to American Embassy in Beirut, Washington, 2 March 1968, Pol. 19, Qatar, NA.
30. Telegram 7072, Rusk to Beirut, Washington, 1 March 1968, Pol. 7, Qatar, NA.
31. Letter, Boyle to Balfour-Paul, 12 March 1968, Doha, FCO 8/723, PRO.
32. Letter, Boyle to Balfour-Paul, Doha, 21 March 1968, FCO 8/723, PRO.
33. Ibid.
34. Letter, Crawford to Stewart, Bahrain, 10 June 1968, pp. 1-3, FCO 8/14, PRO.
35. Letter, Crawford to Weir, Bahrain, 21 March 1968, FCO 8/574, PRO.
36. Letter, Carden to Crawford, Muscat, 4 April 1968, FCO 8/576, PRO.
37. Letter, Carden to Stewart, Muscat, 25 January 1968, FCO 8/574, PRO.
38. Letter, Crawford to Weir, Bahrain, 14 February 1968, FCO 8/574, PRO.
39. Record of a Conversation, Al Ain, 11 April 1968, FCO 8/11, PRO.
40. Letter, Parsons to Stirling, Bahrain, 13 April 1968, FCO 8/11, PRO.
41. Joint Communiqué, Dubai, 27 February 1968, FCO 8/9, PRO.
42. Letter, Roberts to Crawford, Dubai, 6 March 1968, FCO 8/9, PRO.
43. Letter, Weir to Crawford, London, 13 March 1968, FCO 8/9, PRO.
44. Letter, Graham to Weir, Kuwait, 14 March 1968, FCO 8/9, PRO.
45. Letter, Lamb to Crawford, Abu Dhabi, 7 March 1968, FCO 8/9, PRO.
46. Minute, Roberts, Dubai, 4 March 1968, FCO 8/9, PRO.
47. Letter, Boyle to Crawford, Doha, 2 March 1968, FCO 8/9, PRO.
48. Letter, Henderson to Crawford, Abu Dhabi, 13 April 1968, FCO 8/11, PRO.
49. Letter, Henderson to Balfour-Paul, Abu Dhabi, 28 April 1968, FCO 8/11, PRO.
50. Record of a Conversation, Dubai, 16 March 1968, FCO 8/10, PRO.
51. Letter, Henderson to Balfour-Paul, Abu Dhabi, 28 April 1968, FCO 8/11, PRO.
52. Letter, Crawford to Parsons, Bahrain, 8 March 1968, FCO 8/9, PRO.
53. Letter, Foreign Office to Certain Missions, London, 10 April 1968, FCO 8/11, PRO.
54. Ibid.
55. Letter, Crawford to Stewart, Bahrain, 10 June 1968, p. 6, FCO 8/14, PRO.
56. Letter, Crawford to McCarthy, Bahrain, 20 April 1968, FCO 8/11, PRO.
57. Letter, Crawford to Stewart, Bahrain, 10 June 1968, FCO 8/14, PRO.
58. Ibid.
59. Ibid.
60. Airgram 208, Cottam to State Department, Kuwait, 16 May 1968, NEA-10, Pol. 2, KUW, NA.
61. Airgram 226, Cottam to State Department, Kuwait, 29 May 1968, NEA-10, Pol. 2, KUW, NA.
62. Memorandum, Political Resident's Meeting with the Deputy Ruler of Qatar, Doha, 15 June 1968, FCO 8/14, PRO.
63. Record of a Conversation, London, 27 June 1968, FCO 8/15, PRO.
64. Telegram 123, Parsons to Foreign Office, Bahrain, 24 June 1968, FCO 8/14, PRO.
65. Minute, Eyers, London, 1 July 1968, FCO 8/14, PRO.
66. Letter, Parsons to Crawford, Bahrain, 22 July 1968, FCO 8/16, PRO.
67. Minute, Denis, London, 10 July 1968, FCO 8/15, PRO.
68. Memorandum, Allen, London, 10 July 1968, FCO 8/15, PRO.

69.   Letter, Crawford to McCarthy, Bahrain, 2 July 1968, FCO 8/15, PRO.
70.   Letter, Boyle to Balfour-Paul, Doha, 30 June 1968, FCO 8/15, PRO.
71.   Telegram 186, Foreign Office to Commonwealth Office, London, 19 July 1968, FCO 8/16, PRO.
72.   Letter, Arthur to McCarthy, Kuwait, 20 August 1968, FCO 8/638, PRO.
73.   Letter, Carden to McCarthy, Muscat, 31 August 1968, FCO 8/638, PRO.
74.   Letter, Arthur to McCarthy, Kuwait, 3 October 1968, FCO 8/638, PRO.
75.   Letter, McCarthy to Weir, London, 2 October 1968, FCO 8/576, PRO.
76.   Letter, Ward to Weir, Doha, 10 September 1968, FCO 8/16, PRO.
77.   Letter, Weir to Ward, Bahrain, 23 September 1968, FCO 8/16, PRO.
78.   Letter, Bullard to McCarthy, Dubai, 1 October 1968, FCO 8/16, PRO.
79.   Letter, Boyle to Crawford, Doha, 23 November 1968, FCO 8/915/1, PRO.
80.   Letter, Graham to Stewart, Kuwait, 5 November 1968, FCO 8/1030, PRO.
81.   Airgram A-895, Meyer to State Department, Tehran, 4 November 1968, Pol. 2, NA.
82.   Letter, Political Agency to Weir, Doha, 3 December 1968, FCO 8/915/1, PRO.
83.   Letter, Boyle to Weir, Doha, 10 December 1968, FCO 8/915/1, PRO.
84.   Telegram 2866, State Department to American Embassy Jidda, Washington, 12 December 1968, Pol. 7, NA.

7

Countdown to withdrawal

At the beginning of 1969 the proposed union of nine Gulf States, the seven Trucial States, Qatar and Bahrain, still appeared to offer the best hope for the future of the British-protected shaikhdoms. However, meetings of the UAE Council were postponed, initially moved from January to February. Then, Bahrain insisted on further postponement until after the Haj and the Eid Al Adha. Hence, the next meeting of the Provisional Council was scheduled for March. Adviser to the Qatari government Dr Kamal was distressed by the delay and told the Political Agent in Doha that he hoped the practice of indefinite dates 'and even vaguer meeting places' would end: that all of the shaikhdoms would accept an organized calendar and a disciplined program.[1]

Although the Provisional Council had postponed its meetings, in early January the UAE Communications Committee met in Abu Dhabi. None of the delegates on the Committee were specialists in the area of communications, which included navigation as well as civil aviation. The Political Agency in Abu Dhabi reported that Shaikh Zaid's goal was to have the delegates stick strictly to platitudes.[2] Nevertheless, one British optimist suggested HMG continue to promote the UAE. Referring to the rulers, he claimed that 'the more lip service they pay to the Union the harder it will be for them to allow it to collapse.'[3]

Early in the year Qatar's deputy ruler, Shaikh Khalifa bin Hamad Al Thani, visited Iran, which had demanded that a plebiscite be held in Bahrain to determine that shaikhdom's future. All Gulf Arabs were united against the Iranian position and Shaikh Khalifa told his hosts that their attitude toward Bahrain was wrong: that a plebiscite was not in the interest of either the Persians or the Arabs. The visiting Qatari advised the Shah's government immediately to relinquish any claim to Bahrain.[4]

Meanwhile, preparing for Britain's departure, Abu Dhabi's ruler considered how best to enhance his defense and decided to purchase British-made Hunter aircraft. Political Resident Sir Stewart suggested that prior to ordering the Hunters, Shaikh Zaid check with the rulers of Dubai and Qatar. Shaikh Zaid was upset. 'He could not understand why he should take orders from them, nor could he see why he should be bound by their whims or be subject to their domination.' Patiently Sir Stewart explained that defense was not purely an internal matter. All of the rulers were now colleagues in the UAE.[5]

Shaikh Zaid's reluctance to curb his independence was also illustrated by his refusal to check his lavish handouts. Not only did Abu Dhabi's ruler provide gifts to his own tribesmen, he also presented money to tribes living in the territory of other rulers. Sir Stewart claimed to appreciate Shaikh Zaid's motives, but warned that such largesse to individuals 'tended to make the recipients lazy and there was a risk that tribesmen benefiting from his generosity would turn against their own Rulers.'[6]

Kuwait and Oman, too, were concerned about ensuring the security of their territories, but relations between the amirate and the sultanate continued to be cold. Sultan Said still resented Kuwaiti support for Omani rebels and declared that even if Kuwait closed the imamate office in the amirate he would be unwilling to permit a visit from a Kuwaiti emissary. Prior to accepting such a visit, the Sultan demanded evidence that Kuwait had ceased all activity directed against him.[7]

Oman's Sultan was 'already disposed to be unco-operative,' when Whitehall considered how best to approach him about London's intention to withdraw the RAF from its base in Salalah, the Sultan's residence since 1958. Despite occasional lulls, rebel activity in the sultanate had continued and the RAF base in Salalah remained critical to the Sultan's military. As a result, insurgents targeted British forces on that base.[8] In March 1969, a British Intelligence report stated that since Britain's withdrawal from South Arabia the Salalah base no longer had direct value to the RAF.

> Moreover in rebel eyes – and indeed in the eyes of the UN committee on Colonialism and in the eyes of 'progressive socialist nationalist' Arabs worldwide – the Sultanate is a British dependency, the Sultan is a British puppet and the SAF [Sultan's Armed Forces] is a British force. The RAF personnel at Salalah are seen as living proof of this assertion.[9]

Attempting to find a way to leave Salalah without offending Sultan Said, the British Ministry of Defense agreed that if the Sultan deemed it necessary, Britain would increase the number of personnel seconded to the Sultan's forces. However, the Foreign Office did not want seconded officers to become a source of embarrassment. London wished to ascertain that, before becoming involved in any operation, its personnel would seek British approval.[10]

At the end of May, accompanied by Consul General Carden, Sir Stewart visited the Sultan. The Political Resident explained that London had to economize and planned to withdraw the RAF from Salalah, but would remain in Masirah. The Sultan replied that such a withdrawal might serve British interests, but his interests also had to be taken into account; there was no provision in the 1958 agreement between the two countries which allowed Britain to withdraw from Salalah during the period of the lease on Masirah. The terms of the lease permitted him to request a British withdrawal from Salalah, but he had no intention of doing so. Before his guests departed, the Sultan smiled and announced: 'You know, I enjoy a good argument.'[11]

Rebel activity continued. The British commander of the Sultan's Armed Forces Brigadier Purdon did not consider a military solution possible. Nevertheless, he stated that, with more men, 'the position could be held.'[12] Purdon requested that the Sultan agree to increase the size of his force, adding a fourth battalion so that two battalions could be permanently stationed in Dhofar. Purdon also requested that an officer with the rank of colonel be employed to direct operations there and that additional pay be provided to the SAF.[13]

Working with the Sultan was complex, but dealing with Kuwait's ruler was far easier. The new British Ambassador, Sam Falle, reported that Anglo-Kuwaiti relations were businesslike. He saw no evidence of bitterness toward Britain, and only the ruler appeared disturbed about Britain's impending withdrawal. Falle also noted that Kuwaitis were genuinely passionate about Palestine. Although distant from the firing line, they provided substantial financial support to the Fedayeen, and 'Kuwaitis like to think they are in the battle.' Nevertheless, Kuwaitis did not embrace the sizeable population of Palestinian workers living among them. Despite their passion for the Palestinian cause, nationals generally maintained a distance from non-local Arabs. However, as a result of their strong identification with Palestine, Kuwaitis feared the possibility of Israeli reprisal raids. Of course, Kuwaitis had other fears as well. They feared losing their money; they feared Iran and, naturally, they feared Iraq.[14]

During previous assignments, Ambassador Falle had personally kept in touch with opposition movements but, unwilling to alienate the Al Sabah family, he considered it unwise for him to do so in Kuwait. As a result, he encouraged his staff 'to dig deep by discreet means.' Falle enjoyed the intrigue: 'It is a fascinating situation fraught with all sorts of difficulties and dangers, just the way I like it.'[15] In April a member of Falle's staff visited Kuwaiti 'armchair revolutionary', Ahmad Khatib. The Kuwaiti dissident warned that stability in the region could not be based on 'a union of nine unpopular reactionary rulers,' and insisted that Britain was not truly committed to withdrawal: that London would simply move British troops from Bahrain to Muscat and Dhofar. Khatib also claimed that 'Iraq, a progressive country, was too involved in Palestine and in the north to play an effective role in the Gulf.'[16]

Ambassador Falle still considered Iraq to be the most obvious long-term threat to Kuwait. After Britain initially announced its intention to withdraw from the Gulf in 1971, an older Kuwaiti told a British official that 'if you go, Iraq will sooner or later take over.' In June 1969, Falle reported that although Baghdad had extended recognition to Kuwait, there was no reason to assume that Iraq had abandoned its claim. According to Falle, there was some logic in the incorporation of Kuwait in Iraq since 'it is particularly absurd that a minuscule State like Kuwait should have such disproportionate wealth and consequent economic power.'[17]

Strangely, however, the British Ambassador regarded Israel as the most immediate threat to the amirate. He reported that the idea of an Israeli attack might seem 'far-fetched,' nevertheless, since the Kuwaitis made substantial contributions to the Fedayeen, the Israelis might decide to frighten the amirate. In May, the Kuwaiti Chief of General Staff asked Ambassador Falle what Britain would do if Israel launched an attack on Kuwait.[18] No reply appeared necessary after Britain's Ambassador in Tel Aviv, E.J.W. Barnes, assured London that an Israeli attack on Kuwait was unlikely. He affirmed that Israeli officials had not expressed concern about Kuwaiti involvement in the Arab–Israeli conflict, and there was no reason why Israel 'should pick on Kuwait.'[19]

In the spring, the State Department considered potential problems that the United States might face in the Gulf after the British departure. In April, accompanied by a study group, an American admiral called on the Political Agency in Bahrain. The Americans asked if there was a possibility that the British decision to withdraw might be reversed. The Americans also enquired about the stability of the regimes and the economic future of various states. Unimpressed with his American guests, who 'seemed intelligent, attentive and inadequately briefed,' the Political Agent explained that by the end of 1971 the announced withdrawal would proceed without serious difficulty.[20]

At the same time that the American government studied the situation in the Gulf, so too did HMG's Loyal Opposition. Leader of the Conservative Party Edward Heath traveled to the southern Gulf in April. In Bahrain, Heath urged support for the UAE. Shaikh Isa replied that it was difficult for Bahrain to proceed with other states who were totally absorbed in their own affairs or too keen on pleasing Iran.[21] Later, when Heath arrived in Dubai, Shaikh Rashid complained that Britain had provided 'a ridiculously short period' for the British-protected states to learn to protect themselves. During discussions with Heath, the ruler of Dubai conveyed his suspicions of Abu Dhabi's military force and also suggested that Bahrain would not remain a UAE member. Shaikh Rashid claimed that Iran would be more likely to accept Bahrain as an independent state. During Heath's visit to Sharjah, Shaikh Khalid Al Qasimi expressed his deep suspicion of Iran and his fear that the Shah intended to rule the entire Gulf region. Hence, he wanted British troops to remain after 1971.[22]

Heath also visited Saudi Arabia for discussions with King Faisal. The Saudi monarch expressed his support for the UAE, endorsed the concept of a single armed force for the union, and complained that a recent frontier agreement between Abu Dhabi and Qatar had been signed 'behind his back.' Excluding Buraimi, King Faisal had suggested a settlement of the Abu Dhabi/Saudi Arabian frontier, but Shaikh Zaid procrastinated, insisting that a Saudi delegation visit him. According to the Saudi ruler, it was clearly Zaid's responsibility to travel to Riyadh.[23]

King Faisal advised that Britain restrict Shaikh Zaid's purchase of weapons: not refuse to sell him arms but simply procrastinate on the arrangements. He knew that Britain was able to do this 'from his experience with his own defense contracts.' King Faisal also discussed Bahrain and stated unequivocally that the Shah had no claim to that shaikhdom. Turning to the situation in Oman, the Saudi ruler declared that it was impossible to talk with the Sultan and insisted that, before the British left the region, it was essential for them to establish a functioning, secure political system. The King admonished Heath that it was important for the British to avoid the chaos that resulted from Britain's earlier withdrawal from Aden.[24]

Political Resident Sir Stewart Crawford considered it unfortunate that, prior to visiting the shaikhdoms, Heath did not have an opportunity to meet with the Shah and, therefore, during discussions with the rulers, could not speak authoritatively about the Iranian view. But Heath had ample opportunity to hear the perspective of the shaikhs who emphasized that HMG should continue to advise them how best to ensure their future security. Some suggested that Britain offer defense treaties to the shaikhdoms similar to the treaty earlier provided to Kuwait. Heath explained that the treaty with Kuwait had been possible because Britain maintained forces in the region. If similar treaties were provided to the protected states then British troops would have to remain after 1971. The rulers of Bahrain, Dubai, and Sharjah agreed that British forces should stay. Although the ruler of Qatar wished to have a defense treaty with Britain, he was uncertain about whether or not it was necessary for British troops to remain in the region. Abu Dhabi's ruler, too, wanted a defense treaty, but told Heath that once British troops had departed it would be difficult to request their return.[25]

During his tour of the Gulf, Heath also visited Oman and was distressed by how slowly development was progressing. The Sultan, too, now expressed support for a reversal of British policy and did not hesitate to encourage British troops to remain in the region. After listening to the opinions of the rulers, Heath told Sir Stewart that when he returned home he intended to discuss his tour. The Political Resident urged him not to disclose that the rulers wanted British troops to stay on after 1971. Such information might anger Gulf subjects. Heath agreed.[26]

After Heath's departure from Kuwait a British visitor, Sir Dingle Foot, cautioned the Amir that it was not at all clear how Heath could reduce taxes by £400 million and at the same time maintain Britain's military presence in the Middle East. The ruler insisted that Heath would not have suggested remaining in the Gulf if he did not intend to do so. Sir Dingle attempted to explain that, when in opposition, politicians sometimes made promises that they were unable to keep after assuming power. The Amir did not appear to understand that possibility. He was convinced that if the Conservatives took control of the British government they would consult the Gulf rulers and respond favorably to a request to maintain a British military presence in the region.[27]

In an interview on 14 April, Heath said that the British government had undermined its own credibility. During his tour he realized that there was almost universal regret that the British were in fact leaving the Gulf. Nobody had asked the British to leave, and most people I found were completely mystified why the British Labour Government had suddenly decided to abandon the Gulf. Just recall: they sent a Minister round in November 1967 to say the British would stay in the Gulf – would stay – permanently. And only a month later the same Minister had to go round and say the British Government's decided to leave the Gulf.[28]

On 27 April, the *Sunday Times* in London reported that, following his visit to the Gulf, Heath was convinced that it was in Britain's interest to remain in the region.[29] Arabian Department officials were not pleased with Heath's remarks. Clearly, a Conservative administration could not be certain of what to do until it achieved office. Foreign Office officials also worried that talk of a reversal of policy might cause problems.[30] A British decision to remain in the Gulf would likely inflame revolutionary activity. Minister of State for Foreign Affairs Goronwy Roberts declared that 'the balance of argument is heavily against reversal of policy.' Rather than remain in the Gulf after 1971, Roberts suggested that Britain concentrate on assisting the organization of a viable defense for the shaikhdoms: a system that would include equipment and personnel on contract. According to Roberts:

> We should be more explicit about the 'technical assistance' we are prepared to offer in training and officer personnel. All this is not a defense commitment or a partial reversal of our decision to pull out; but it could reassure the sheikhs.[31]

During the summer, Political Agent in Abu Dhabi Charles Treadwell became increasingly uneasy about what he considered to be the shaikhdom's deteriorating political and economic situation. Contractors and others owed money were not being paid. Treadwell faulted the long absences of Shaikh Zaid, who spent considerable time outside of Abu Dhabi, his 'real centre of affairs.' Treadwell also noted that when the ruler returned to his capital he lived with the expatriate community. The Political Agent told the ruler that to keep in touch with his subjects he ought to reinstate a regular *majlis*. Shaikh Zaid claimed that he was too busy. Treadwell replied that other rulers were also busy, but made time for the customary *majlis*. The ruler insisted that more than a regular *majlis* was necessary, he needed something that apparently money could not buy: efficient senior officials who spoke Arabic. The Political Agent agreed that the absence of appropriate officials was a problem. For example, Abu Dhabi's radio station was controlled by Palestinians. These Palestinians served their own cause rather than the interests of the shaikhdom. 'The station could be appropriately called Sawt Arafat.' To resolve the problem, Treadwell advised that Shaikh Zaid hire a firm of management consultants, and in order to soothe the shaikhs who now served as department chairmen he could appoint them ministers without executive power.[32]

As British officials and ruling shaikhs pondered how best to plan for the future, still obsessed with a possible Israeli threat, Ambassador Falle suggested that one Israeli airplane might destroy most of Kuwait's desalination and power complexes. However, again Falle had to admit that despite Iraqi recognition of Kuwait and the considerable financial assistance Kuwait offered Baghdad, Iraq presented a more serious long-term danger. According to Falle, the Iraqi threat was not immediate. Nevertheless, there was 'no reason why Iraq should have abandoned her hopes of absorbing Kuwait one day.'[33] Meanwhile, the Saudis and Kuwaitis agreed to establish a single border between them: a border that would replace the Neutral Zone established by the 1922 Treaty of Uqair. The new border did not affect the ownership of resources. However, Saudi officials perceived yet another threat to Kuwait. British representatives in Jedda reported that the Saudis were irritated by Kuwait's 'flirtation with such dangerous innovations as parliaments, elections and trade unions.' Nevertheless, Falle speculated that if, once again, Iraq attempted to take Kuwait, King Faisal would send moral and military assistance to the amirate.[34]

In the spring of 1969, the Al Sabahs appeared to be absorbed in efforts to safeguard their country from domestic threats, students, and trade union activists who agitated for liberalization. Taking action that probably gladdened the Saudi ruling family, special courts were set up to deal with suspected activists. Many young men were arrested and it was generally accepted that those arrested were beaten and insulted. Ambassador Falle considered establishment of the new courts a serious mistake. He speculated that Kuwaiti authorities ought to have simply approached the fathers of suspected students and told them to keep their sons in line.[35]

While heavy-handed at home, the Al Sabahs agreed to assist with the training of new diplomats from the shaikhdoms that had heretofore relied on HMG. In 1949, Britain had set up a course to train Indian diplomats; a course that later also accepted both Pakistani and Sri Lankan students. However, in 1964, there were few applicants from Commonwealth countries. As a result, the course for

Commonwealth diplomats ceased and individual applications for training were treated on merit. At the beginning of 1969, Bahrain requested British assistance to train members for its diplomatic corp. The Foreign Office did not consider the old course for students from Commonwealth countries suitable. Earlier, Kuwait had assisted the Bahrainis to establish a Ministry of External Affairs. Whitehall considered it sensible for Gulf Arabs to be trained by other Arabs. One British official asked, 'Since the Kuwaitis are willing to help, is there any real wisdom in encouraging the Bahrainis to continue leaning on a Britain which will not be Bahrain's prop and mainstay after 1971 as it is now?'[36]

Kuwaitis agreed that their training would be preferable for the future diplomats of the Gulf region.[37] Meanwhile, Qatar's deputy ruler, Shaikh Khalifa, wanted his county's future diplomats to learn English and acquire a broad general education. He sent approximately thirty young men abroad to various institutions, most to Europe, but 'one or two only to Cairo (for the look of it) and none at all to Baghdad.'[38]

Rulers of the nine states met in Doha on 10 May 1969. Political Resident Sir Stewart Crawford reported that distrust between the rulers of Bahrain and Qatar was evident. Although lacking wealth, Bahrain had a far bigger population, and one that was better educated.[39] The Qatari deputy ruler was disappointed about what he perceived to be diminishing hopes for union. Shaikh Khalifa Al Thani was now convinced that until Iran's claim to Bahrain was resolved it would be impossible to form an effective union that included his state. However, if the critical problem of the Iranian claim to Bahrain could be resolved, the next hurdle would be the Bahraini desire to run the union. Although Bahrain had no money, and could not make a sizeable economic contribution, Bahrain's delegation to meetings of the nine had caused obstructions whenever it appeared that Bahrain would not have its way. The Qatari deputy ruler concluded that the best way to proceed would be to begin with the union of the seven Trucial States. Qatar would then join Abu Dhabi, but as a military ally only. At the same time, Shaikh Khalifa Al Thani would attempt functional cooperation among the eight in areas that were not politically vital. According to Political Agent Henderson:

> He would include Bahrain to some extent in this functional cooperation, and he said magnanimously and with no hint of a smile that he would be prepared, for example, to lend Bahrain money for specific projects within Bahrain, e.g. health, education, etc. (I succeeded

in suppressing my urge to laugh at this point; but the thought of Bahrain being lent money by Qatar to build schools was almost too much). This was purely for my benefit, and I cannot see this ever happening.[40]

Henderson attempted to convince Qatar's deputy ruler that a union of nine still remained the best solution, that it was unwise for Qatar to contemplate standing alone. Officially, Qatar remained an advocate of the union of nine, but it was clear that Shaikh Khalifa Al Thani had

an unshakable private resolve not to join a Union which contains Bahrain, but he does not want to be blamed for pushing Bahrain out; and it would be wrong to quote this as being his view yet. Officially, and in effect, he is still a strong niner.[41]

At the same time, Qatar's ruler, Ahmed Al Thani, was convinced that the union of nine 'will never be.' However, when asked what would happen after the British departure, 'he shrugs his shoulders and looks in bored expectation that the interview will soon end.'[42]

By the summer of 1969, prospects for a UAE that included all nine shaikhdoms appeared dim. Political Resident Sir Stewart did not want the rulers to reproach Britain for failure of the union. 'It is for them to face the music if they give it up. We should give no cause for blame to fall on us, if we can help it.' Sir Stewart maintained that it remained possible that Iran would settle its dispute with Bahrain. At the same time, he doubted that Doha would be able to stand up to Saudi pressure if the Saudis decided that they did not want to see inclusion of Qatar in the union.[43]

In July, Qatar's deputy ruler visited London. Prior to his visit, the Political Agency in Doha requested that a senior official meet with him because 'he takes it badly if the person who meets him is not important enough in his view.'[44] During discussions with Minister of State Goronwy Roberts, Shaikh Khalifa stated that although Qatar was doing all that was possible, the union of nine was not working, nor did he consider it likely that it would be able to work in the future. Now he wished to look at the possibility of a union of eight, a union which excluded Bahrain. The Qatari argued that in addition to the Iranian claim to Bahrain there were two more problems. The other shaikhdoms continued to fear possible Bahraini domination and also worried that Bahrain might take too large a portion of UAE resources. Roberts disagreed with Shaikh Khalifa's assessment and continued to encourage a union of nine.[45]

While in London, Qatar's deputy ruler wanted to interview

candidates for the post of Commander of the Qatari Airforce, a force consisting of four small aircraft. From Doha, Political Agent Henderson warned the Foreign Office that Shaikh Khalifa 'always tries to get things on the cheap – with disastrous results in his security forces.' Henderson requested that officials in London attempt to persuade the Qatari leader that it was unwise to hire airforce personnel who lacked the highest qualifications.[46]

Soon after Shaikh Khalifa Al Thani's visit to London the ruler of Sharjah, Shaikh Khalid bin Muhammad Al Qasimi, arrived. Meeting with Goronwy Roberts, Shaikh Khalid Al Qasimi predicted disaster if union did not succeed. Roberts told Sharjah's ruler that HMG was ready to provide assistance but would not impose union. Hence, the success of the venture depended upon the rulers themselves. Shaikh Khalid emphasized his fears that, after Britain withdrew, Iran would take Sharjah's Abu Musa Island, territory that was not his personal property, but that belonged to his people. Roberts suggested that Shaikh Khalid directly contact the Shah and discuss the issue, ruler to ruler.[47]

Reporting from Bahrain in the middle of July, Political Resident Crawford said that all the rulers were increasingly concerned that the period prior to Britain's military withdrawal was rapidly drawing to a close. Since it appeared that the union of nine might break down and Bahrain be excluded, Crawford wished to do what was possible to give the union of eight the best possible chance of success. In the event that Qatar was unwilling to participate in a union of eight, a union of the seven Trucial States remained a possibility, and had the support of the population of these seven shaikhdoms, 'which feels little in common with either Bahrain or Qatar.' In addition, the seven Trucial States already had a working Trucial States Council and the Trucial Oman Scouts. Since Shaikh Zaid's expenditures had temporarily outstripped his resources, Abu Dhabi's ruler appeared more willing to cooperate with his neighbors. However, there was the possibility that, given their quarrel with Abu Dhabi over territory, the Saudis might oppose a union of seven in which Shaikh Zaid had a prominent role.[48]

Although the union of nine still appeared to be, at least in theory, the best solution, it was not now realistic. Sir Stewart concluded that even if Kuwait and Saudi Arabia joined Britain in encouraging the union of nine, there was little possibility of success. Hence, 'we must set our sights lower and aim only at averting if we can its open collapse.' Nevertheless, the Political Resident continued to advise that, as before, Britain express support for the union of nine.

> We should accept that if it proves impossible to save the Union of Nine, the Union of Eight would be the best fall-back aim, and, provided it is first shown that this solution is acceptable to the Rulers and the other neighbouring Arab countries, we should back it and a separate Bahrain. Whichever way we go, we should seek to ensure that the decision is seen to be that of the Arab Governments concerned, and not of our contriving.[49]

Ruler of Bahrain, Shaikh Isa bin Sulman Al Khalifa, visited London in August, together with his brother, deputy ruler Shaikh Khalifa bin Sulman Al Khalifa, 'who is for all intents and purposes the Head of the Bahrain Government.'[50] Minister of State Roberts attempted to assure the Bahrainis that the Shah would be reasonable. But Shaikh Khalifa bin Sulman was doubtful. Iran still refused to recognize the existence of the government of Bahrain, and the deputy ruler anticipated trouble. Shaikh Khalifa Al Khalifa also noted that the other Gulf States feared upsetting the Shah and, therefore, did nothing to support Bahrain. Roberts stated that once the Iranian claims to Bahrain had been resolved, the development of the union would progress. Now Head of Bahrain's Department of Foreign Affairs and Information, Shaikh Mohammed bin Mubarak bin Hamad, who had accompanied the ruler and deputy ruler, suggested that the UAE ought to accept a Catholic rather than a Muslim marriage so that no withdrawal be permitted.[51]

After his visit to London, the Bahraini ruler also visited Washington. Shaikh Isa had been reluctant to go to the United States and only agreed to the trip under pressure from his brother and the Bahrain Petroleum Company. Prior to the trip, Bahrain's ruler was informed that he would be met by a State Department official, but would not meet the Secretary of State. Shaikh Isa was concerned with his status. However, considering the future of the Gulf region, deputy ruler Shaikh Khalifa Al Khalifa insisted that it was more important for Bahrain to make contact with the government of the United States than to worry about the level at which the ruler was received.[52]

British officials, too, were interested in what sort of role the United States would assume. From the beginning of 1969, the British Embassy in Washington paid close attention to how the new administration of President Richard Nixon viewed the American role in the Gulf. It appeared that some Americans in the Department of Defense wanted to 'beef up' the US Naval force in the Gulf (COMIDEASTFOR) after Britain's departure, but British Embassy officials in Washington speculated that advocates of an increased

American presence would find stiff opposition in Congress. In addition, if Washington increased its presence in the Gulf, the Soviets would likely demand equivalent facilities.[53]

Unfortunately, British policy had recently changed and the State Department was no longer informed about the exchanges that took place between Gulf rulers and HMG. 'Our "lack of trust" is referred to very frequently at desk level, although more in sorrow than in anger.' British officials in Washington cautioned the Foreign Office to remember that after Britain left the Gulf, it might be essential to rely on Americans to protect British nationals and support British interests. 'To freeze the Americans out now may cost us much-needed goodwill in the future.'[54]

British officials in Washington continued to report American resistance to assuming additional military responsibility. It appeared that influential Missouri senator Stuart Symington was 'on the war-path' against a larger American military commitment abroad. A staff member on the Senate Foreign Relations Committee told his British contacts that, at present, it would be imprudent for the Nixon administration to attempt to raise the possibility of expanding COMIDEASTFOR.[55]

Regardless of Washington's position, Shaikh Zaid was optimistic about the future. As a result, the Abu Dhabi ruler permitted his exiled brother, Shaikh Shakhbut, to return home. After more than three years in exile, Shakhbut landed in Abu Dhabi. He was greeted at the airport by thousands of tribesmen from Al Ain and Liwa. These men came to pay respect to their former ruler. Together with his brother, Shaikh Zaid, Shaikh Shakhbut moved through the crowd. Some of the older Bedu knelt at their former ruler's feet. Excitement reached such heights that after the shaikhs entered the airport VIP lounge, crowds pressed against the door, breaking several panes of glass. In a brief scuffle that followed, 'an over-zealous policeman' punched Abu Dhabi's Assistant Political Agent, Anthony Reeve, in the stomach. The day after his arrival in Abu Dhabi, Shaikh Shakhbut retired to the new palace in Al Ain, which his brother, the ruler, had built for him. That very day, Shaikh Zaid left Abu Dhabi for a holiday. According to Reeve:

> It is a measure of Zaid's self-confidence that Shakhbut should be back in the country which he ruled for almost forty years and that the present Ruler should set off on the very next day for a month's hunting in Pakistan leaving the Government in the hands of his son.[56]

In December, the Political Agents met to review the year. Iran's claim to Bahrain had yet to be resolved and Bahrain's membership in the UAE appeared unlikely. At the same time, the Political Agents discussed the possibility that Bahrainis might pursue some form of union with Kuwait. They concluded, however, that the Saudis would oppose such an arrangement and that Kuwaitis, too, might object because many considered Bahrain 'ripe for revolution.' The relationship of Qatar to the UAE was also discussed. It appeared that the ruler and deputy ruler were neither firmly opposed nor firmly in favor of the union. As for Abu Dhabi, Shaikh Zaid was disappointed with the lack of progress toward the union of nine but remained committed to its establishment. Sharjah's ruler, Shaikh Khalid Al Qasimi, agreed and expressed willingness to do what was necessary to assist in bringing union to fruition. Dubai ruler, Shaikh Rashid, now showed little enthusiasm for the union, and the ruler of Ras al Khaimah, Shaikh Saqr Al Qasimi, was convinced that the union was no longer a possibility.[57]

The future of the region continued to remain uncertain. At the conclusion of 1969 there were still numerous possibilities, even the possibility that a new British government might defer withdrawal. Gulf rulers continued to search for solutions that would ensure the security of their shaikhdoms and the prosperity of their people.

NOTES

1.   Letter, Boyle to Weir, Doha, 6 January 1969, FCO 8/916, PRO.
2.   Letter, Treadwell to Weir, Abu Dhabi, 6 January 1969, FCO 8/916, PRO.
3.   Minute, Eyers, London, 21 January 1969, FCO 8/927/1, PRO.
4.   Letter, Boyle to Weir, Doha, 18 January 1969, FCO 8/1162, PRO.
5.   Record of a Conversation between the Political Resident and Shaikh Zaid, Al-Ain, 24 February 1969, PRO.
6.   Ibid.
7.   Letter, Carden to Graham, Muscat, 5 January 1969, FCO 8/1042, PRO.
8.   Joint Intelligence Staff, Possible Effects on RAF Salalah arising from Threats to the Sultan in Dhofar, 10 March 1969, FCO 8/1089, PRO.
9.   Ibid.
10.   Letter, Davenport to Goulty, London, 15 May 1969, FCO 8/1089, PRO.
11.   Note, Crawford, 7 June 1969, FCO 8/1089, PRO.
12.   Note, Adler, London, 19 December 1969, FCO 8/1088, PRO.
13.   Letter, Adler to West, London, 22 December 1969, FCO 8/1088, PRO.
14.   Letter, Falle to Stewart, Kuwait, 12 March 1969, FCO 8/1027, PRO.
15.   Letter, Falle to McCarthy, Kuwait, 24 March 1969, FCO 8/1027, PRO.
16.   Minute, Brehony, London, 4 April 1969, FCO 8/1027, PRO.
17.   Letter, Falle to Stewart, Arabia, 27 May 1969, FCO 8/1027, PRO.

18. Ibid.
19. Letter, Barnes to Tripp, Tel Aviv, 18 June 1969, FCO 8/1027, PRO.
20. Letter, Stirling to McCarthy, Bahrain, 15 April 1969, FCO 8/935, PRO.
21. Letter, Stirling to Crawford, Bahrain, 8 April 1969, FCO 8/979, PRO.
22. Letter, Bullard to Weir, Dubai, 5 April 1969, FCO 8/979, PRO.
23. Letter, Tatham to Arabian Department, Jedda, 9 April 1969, FCO 8/979, PRO.
24. Ibid.
25. Letter, Crawford to McCarthy, Bahrain, 9 April 1969, FCO 8/979, PRO.
26. Letter, Crawford to McCarthy, Bahrain, 9 April 1969, FCO 8/979, PRO.
27. Letter, Falle to Edes, Kuwait, 7 April 1969, FCO 8/979, PRO.
28. Interview with Edward Heath, 14 April 1969, FCO 8/979, PRO.
29. Memorandum, Arabian Department, London, 2 May 1969, FCO 8/979, PRO.
30. Ibid.
31. Memorandum, Roberts, London, 26 June 1969, FCO 8/979, PRO.
32. Letter, Treadwell to Crawford, Abu Dhabi, 4 August 1969, FCO 8/1211, PRO.
33. Letter, Falle to Stewart, Arabia, 27 May 1969, FCO 8/1027, PRO.
34. Letter, Morris to McCarthy, Jedda, 10 June 1969, FCO 8/1027, PRO.
35. Letter, Blatherwick to Ibbott, 4 June 1969, FCO 8/1027, PRO.
36. Letter, McCarthy to Everard, London, 9 June 1969, FCO 8/1013, PRO.
37. Letter, Goodison to McCarthy, Kuwait, 24 June 1969, FCO 8/1013, PRO.
38. Letter, Henderson to Everard, Doha, 24 June 1969, FCO 8/1013, PRO.
39. Letter, Crawford to Stewart, Bahrain, 15 July 1969, FCO 8/920/1, PRO.
40. Letter, Henderson to Everard, Doha, 23 June 1969, FCO 8/919, PRO.
41. Ibid.
42. Ibid.
43. Telegram 249, Crawford to Foreign Office, Bahrain, 8 July 1969, FCO 8/919, PRO.
44. Letter, Henderson to Battiscombe, Doha, 24 June 1969, FCO 8/1163, PRO.
45. Letter, McCarthy to Crawford, London, 10 July 1969, FCO 8/1163, PRO.
46. Letter, Henderson to Battiscombe, Doha, 10 June 1969, FCO 8/1163, PRO.
47. Record of a Meeting, London, 31 July 1969, FCO 8/1279/1, PRO.
48. Letter, Crawford to Stewart, Bahrain, 15 July 1969, FCO 8/920/1, PRO.
49. Letter, Crawford to Stewart, Bahrain, 15 July 1969, FCO 8/920/1, PRO.
50. Minute, McCarthy, Visit of the Ruler of Bahrain, London, 14 August 1969, FCO 8/1026/1, PRO.
51. Record of a Conversation, London, 27 August 1969, FCO 8/1026/1, PRO.
52. Letter, Stirling to Battiscombe, Bahrain, 16 July 1969, FCO 8/1026/1, PRO.
53. Letter, Dean to Gore-Booth, Washington, 8 January 1969, FCO 8/935, PRO.
54. Ibid.
55. Letter, Urwick to Acland, Washington, 12 February 1969, FCO 8/935, PRO.
56. Letter, Reeve to Weir, Abu Dhabi, 20 December 1969, FCO 8/1276/1, PRO.
57. Political Agents' Conference, 3–5 December 1969, FCO 8/926/1, PRO.

Conclusion

In March 1970, at the request of the Shah, the Secretary General of the United Nations sent a mission of inquiry to Bahrain. The mission was required to ascertain if the inhabitants of the shaikhdom wanted independence or preferred Iranian rule. The vast majority of Bahrainis declared their desire for a completely independent sovereign state.[1] At the same time, Sharjah and Iran reached an understanding on the disputed island of Abu Musa. Both countries agreed that if oil was discovered on the island they would share the revenue. In addition, the Shah promised to provide financial assistance to Sharjah.[2]

Now Bahrain wanted an increased American presence in the Gulf. According to the Bahraini Director of Foreign Affairs, Shaikh Mohammed bin Mubarak, Bahrain was under Soviet pressure to establish closer ties. Hence, although his government appreciated relations with the American Consul in Dhahran, 'in changed circumstances US should have permanent office in Bahrain, either consulate or trade office.' Assistant Secretary of State Joseph Sisco told the Bahraini Director of Foreign Affairs that the United States had remained in the background. However, Washington considered it vital that the future shape of the region be established before Britain's departure. Secretary Sisco expressed confidence that the Shah wished to be helpful and that the Saudi monarch, too, wanted stability in the region. At the same time, Sisco cautioned, 'We want to help if our help is wanted but do not want to import cold war into area.'[3]

Prior to the June 1970 British elections, Political Resident Sir Stewart Crawford suggested to an American official that Gulf rulers were most likely hoping that the Conservatives could deliver them from the awesome responsibilities of independence. At the same time, the Director of Bahraini Foreign Affairs stated that while it was necessary to end the colonial relationship with Britain and establish a new relationship between independent 'adult' states, there was no reason for Britain to relinquish its Gulf base.[4]

Meanwhile, Conservative Party leaders continued to proclaim their opposition to the Labour government's decision to leave the Gulf. Therefore, after the Conservative Party achieved victory, it seemed likely that plans for withdrawal would be discarded. However, both Iran and Saudi Arabia adamantly opposed the continuation of Britain's presence in the Gulf. Unwilling to offend its more powerful neighbors, Kuwait, too, declared that after 1971 HMG would no longer be welcome. Of course, given such opposition, the Trucial States Qatar and Bahrain now hesitated to offend Arab nationalism by admitting that they still favored a British presence.[5]

Since the prospect of British withdrawal brought 'an air of uneasiness to the Gulf,' Washington looked at how best to ensure the stability of the region. At this juncture, the United States did not consider replacing the British presence with an American presence. A State Department memorandum stated that while Gulf rulers were concerned about possible Soviet encroachment, they most feared radical Arabism. According to Washington, Iran was the most powerful and stable state in the region and was willing to assume the role of guardian of the Gulf. Despite a long history of Arab/Persian antagonism, inflamed by Persian reluctance to 'conceal their belief that Arabs are inferior,' the State Department considered Iran likely to serve as a stabilizing force.[6]

Since Iran already had a formidable military capacity, as well as substantial oil revenue and manpower, it appeared that the Shah's government could successfully undertake the task:

> Having foregone its claim to Bahrain, it has begun assiduously to woo its Gulf Arab neighbors by invitation to Tehran, the dispatch of special envoys and good will missions, and the offer of financial and technical aid. It has talked quietly with its largest Arab neighbor, Saudi Arabia, about military cooperation and steps Iran might take to come to Saudi aid in time of emergency.[7]

Saudi King Faisal appeared satisfied with Iranian policy. During a brief visit to Dubai on 7 June he spoke to the six Trucial State rulers. The Saudi monarch praised Iran's decision to relinquish its claim to Bahrain. In addition, he criticized rumors of a secret Iranian/Saudi pact that had been circulating in the region. According to King Faisal, such rumors were designed only to create ill feeling among the states of the area.[8]

While Iran prepared for its new role and London briefly hesitated about whether to go or to stay, HMG took steps to ensure the future of Oman. With British assistance, in July 1970, Sayyid Qaboos bin Said toppled his father. The deposed Sultan departed Oman and settled in London's Dorchester Hotel. Immediately, the new Sultan of Oman, Sultan Qaboos, began the work of building a modern state. As a result, Omanis living in exile returned home. Three months later Qatar's Director of Immigration reported that approximately two hundred Omanis living in Doha had left for Oman. He anticipated that more would follow. However, he asserted that this migration would not affect his country because all of the Omanis had been manual laborers and there was 'an inexhaustible supply of Pakistanis, Baluchis, Turkomans, etc. to take their place.'[9]

At the end of July, Foreign Secretary Sir Alec Douglas Home appointed retired diplomat Sir William Luce to be his special representative to investigate the situation in the Gulf region. Two months after his appointment, Sir William reported that postponement of HMG's withdrawal would not serve the interests of either Britain or the Gulf States.[10] Plans for withdrawal continued to move forward. The British government announced that, on 1 December 1971, its obligations under the earlier treaties of protection would cease.

As the countdown to British withdrawal continued, American officials in the Gulf region maintained contact with the ruling shaikhs. In October 1970, Bahraini ruler Shaikh Isa appeared doubtful that Sir William Luce's efforts to unite the shaikhdoms would succeed. Referring to the shaikhs of the Lower Gulf, Shaikh Isa told a visiting American that 'they cannot read or write, they are Bedus.'[11] And later, looking back on Britain's tenure in his region, Shaikh Zaid claimed, 'The tragedy remains, however, that for the duration of its stay here Britain did not prepare the area or its people for independence of any sort.'[12]

Finally, on 14 August 1971, Bahrain declared its independence and applied for membership in the United Nations. Qatar soon followed and both newly independent states signed Treaties of Friendship with Britain.

> The eagerness for separate status manifested by Bahrain and Qatar reflected their consciousness of being 'superior' to the seven smaller shaykhdoms: and mini-states were no longer a rarity in the world as a whole.[13]

As British protection ended, six of the Trucial States – Abu Dhabi, Dubai, Sharjah, Ajman, Umm Al Qawain, Fujariah – finally succeeded in forming the United Arab Emirates. On 2 December, ruler of Abu Dhabi Shaikh Zaid was sworn in as first President and Britain immediately concluded a Treaty of Friendship with the new nation; a treaty similar to those earlier concluded with Bahrain and Qatar after both had opted for independence rather than UAE membership.

Ruler of Ras Al Khaimah Shaikh Saqr bin Mohammed Al Qasimi had earlier refused to join the UAE and did not do so until February 1972. 'The odd man out' Shaikh Saqr wanted a position that he was unable to achieve – equal status with the more powerful states within the union, Abu Dhabi and Dubai. Hence, he continued to search for oil and gas. In addition, he also established his own mini-army, composed of 250 men, and he set up a miniature naval unit equipped with four rubber dinghies.[14]

Prior to departure, Britain had repeatedly advised the rulers to settle their differences with one another and with their more powerful neighbors. However, not all differences were resolved. Shortly before British protection ended, on 30 November, Iran sent troops to occupy a portion of Abu Musa. The Iranians were greeted warmly by official representatives of Shaikh Saqr bin Sultan Al Qasim.[15] However, Iran also seized two small islands in the straits of Hormuz – the Greater and Lesser Tunbs - which had previously been claimed by Ras Al Khaimah. Ruler of Ras al Khaimah Shaikh Saqr bin Mohammad Al Qasimi maintained a small police force on the Greater Tunb. Tehran reported that this force fired on Iranian troops, killing one officer. Ras Al Khaimah, too, suffered casualties.[16] The Shah 'was allowed to get away with this tweaking of the lion's tail.' Despite Baghdad's earlier attempt to take Kuwait, now posing as protector of the Gulf Arab States, Iraq suspended diplomatic relations with Britain.[17]

Embarrassed by the Iranian use of force during Britain's final moment in the region, *The Times* blamed the victim, claiming that Shaikh Saqr should have worked out a peaceful settlement with the Iranians and had 'only himself to blame' for the invasion.

Thus ended yet another chapter in Great Britain's imperial history. HMG's long period of dominance in the region came to a less than glorious conclusion. However, despite Shaikh Zaid's appraisal, Britain had attempted to assist in preparing a foundation for modern nation-states. The newly independent states continued to develop, to work in harmony with each other, and to play a role in the wider Arab world. Although after independence the Gulf States were unable to achieve military self-sufficiency, while relying on western assistance they continued efforts to contribute to their own defense. At the same time, relations between HMG and the shaikhs of the Gulf region remained firm.

NOTES

1. J.B. Kelly, *Arabia, the Gulf and the West* (New York: Basic Books, 1980), pp. 58–9.
2. *The Times*, 9 December 1971, p. 2.
3. Telegram, Rogers to State Department, Dhahran, 14 May 1970, Pol. 7, Bahrain, NA.
4. Telegram 735, American Consul to Secretary of State, Dhahran, 1 June, 1970, Pol. 33, NA.
5. Kelly, *Arabia, the Gulf and the West*, pp. 79–80.
6. Memorandum for Henry Kissinger, Washington, 5 June 1970, Pol. 33, Persian Gulf, NA.
7. Ibid.
8. Telegram 2422, Embassy to Secretary of State, Tehran, 8 June 1970, Pol. 33, Persian Gulf, NA.
9. Enclosure to Airgram A-87, p. 4, American Consul to Secretary of State, Dhahran, 21 October 1970, Pol. 19, FAA, NA.
10. Kelly, *Arabia, the Gulf and the West*, p. 82.
11. Enclosure to Airgram A-87, p. 1, American Consul to Secretary of State, Dhahran, 21 October 1970, Pol. 19, FAA, NA.
12. Claud Morris, *The Desert Falcon* (London: Morris International, 1976), p. 95.
13. Glen Balfour-Paul, *The End of Empire in the Middle East* (Cambridge: Cambridge University Press, 1991), p. 131.
14. *The Times*, 21 December 1971, p. v.
15. *The Times*, 9 December 1971, p. 2.
16. *The Times*, 1 December 1971, p. 8.
17. Frank Brenchley, *Britain and the Middle East: An Economic History, 1945–87* (London: Lester Crook, 1989), p. 172.

Index